Book Sense 76 selection — November/December 2001.

Los Angeles Times "Discoveries" selection, October 2001.

The novelist Arundhati Roy ... has emerged as India's most impassioned critic of globalization.

— *New York Times*

Arundhati Roy's essays evoke a stark image of two Indias being driven "resolutely in opposite directions," a small India on its way to a "glittering destination" while the rest "melts into the darkness and disappears"—a microcosm of much of the world, she observes, though "in India your face is slammed right up against it." Traced with sensitivity and skill, the unfolding picture is interlaced with provocative reflections on the writer's mission and burden, and inspiring accounts of the "spectacular struggles" of popular movements that "refuse to lie down and die." Another impressive work by a fine writer.

— Noam Chomsky

Writers have proved when they turn their back to power and start to feel the pulse and pain of society, they become powerful. This is the power beyond power that Arundhati Roy brings forth in *Power Politics*.

—Vandana Shiva

Arundhati Roy combines her brilliant style as a novelist with her powerful commitment to social justice in producing these eloquent, penetrating essays.

—Howard Zinn

POWER

POLITICS

SECOND EDITION

ARUNDHATI ROY

SOUTH END PRESS
CAMBRIDGE, MASSACHUSETTS

Cover photograph: August 1999: A woman bathes next to the half-submerged temple at Khoteswar, a village on the banks of the Narmada river. The temple was in use until a couple of years ago but has since been submerged due to a rise in water level, a direct result of the Sardar Sarovar Dam. Photograph by Karen Robinson.

Second edition. First printing.

Library of Congress Cataloging-in-Publication Data

Roy, Arundhati.
Power politics / Arundhati Roy. — 2nd ed.
  p. cm.
  Includes bibliographical references and index.
  ISBN 0-89608-669-0 (cloth) — ISBN 0-89608-668-2 (pbk.)
  1. India — politics and government — 1977– I. Title.

JQ231 .R69 2001
320.954—dc21

South End Press, 7 Brookline Street, #1
Cambridge, MA 02139-4146
www.southendpress.org

05 04 03 02 01   1 2 3 4 5

PRINTED IN CANADA

TABLE OF CONTENTS

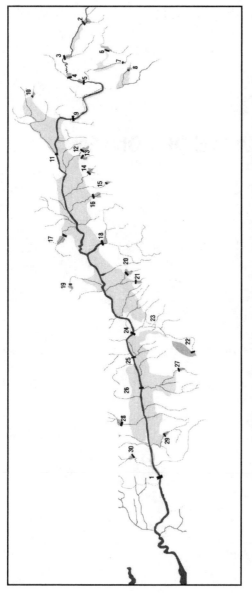

Map of Proposed Big Dams in the Narmada valley. 1: Sardar Sarovar, 2: Upper Narmada, 3: Raghavpur, 4: Rosara, 5: Singarpur, 6: Upper Burhner, 7: Halon, 8: Matiari, 9: Bargi, 10: Bargi, 11: Ataria, 11: Chinki, 12: Sher, 13: Machherva, 14: Shakkar, 15: Siterawa, 16: Dudhi, 17: Barna, 18: Tawa, 19: Kolar, 20: Morand, 21: Ganjal, 22: Sukta, 23: Punassa Lift, 24: Indira Sagar, 25: Omkareshwar, 26: Maheshwar, 27: Upper Veda, 28: Maan, 29: Lower Goi, 30: Jobat. Map by Ian Nixon and *New Internationalist*, courtesy of Maggie Black. Additional production by Christopher Mattison.

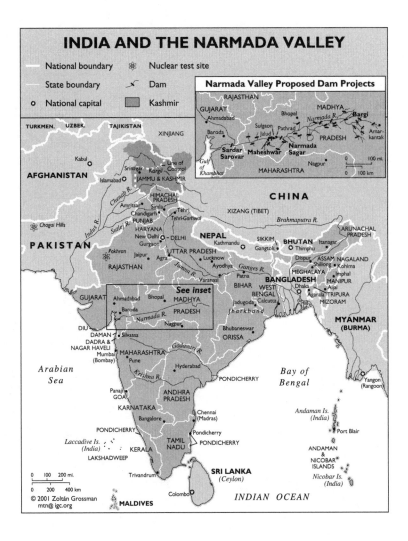

INDIA AND THE NARMADA VALLEY

— National boundary ※ Nuclear test site

— State boundary ⤳ Dam

o National capital ▢ Kashmir

Narmada Valley Proposed Dam Projects

RAJASTHAN

GUJARAT Bhopal MADHYA Bargi

Ahmadabad Narmada R. Amar-

Baroda Sulgaon Pathrad PRADESH kantak

Jalud

Sardar Narmada

Sarovar Maheshwar Sagar

Gulf Nagpur 0 100 mi.

of MAHARASHTRA 0 100 km

Khambhat

TURKMEN. UZBEK. TAJIKISTAN

XINJIANG

Kabul o Line of CHINA

Srinagar Control

Islamabad o Kargil

AFGHANISTAN JAMMU & KASHMIR

Chenab R.

HIMACHAL

Amritsar PRADESH

Chagai Hills Chandigarh Simla Tehri XIZANG (TIBET) Brahmaputra R.

Sutlej R. PUNJAB Tehri-Garhwal

HARYANA ARUNACHAL

PAKISTAN New Delhi o—DELHI NEPAL PRADESH

Gurgaon Kathmandu SIKKIM BHUTAN Itanagar

Pokhran UTTAR PRADESH Gangtok Thimphu ASSAM NAGALAND

Jaipur Agra Lucknow Dispur Shillong Kohima

RAJASTHAN Ayodhya Ganges R. MEGHALAYA Imphal

Patna BANGLADESH MANIPUR

Varanasi BIHAR Dhaka Aijal

Indus R. Jamna R. WEST Agarala TRIPURA

See inset BENGAL MIZORAM

GUJARAT Bhopal MADHYA Jadugoda Calcutta

Ahmadabad PRADESH Jharkhand MYANMAR

Baroda (BURMA)

DIU Narmada R. Nagpur Bhubaneswar

DAMAN Silvassa Godavari R. ORISSA

DADRA &

NAGAR HAVELI Mumbai MAHARASHTRA

Arabian (Bombay) Pune Yangon

Sea Hyderabad Bay of (Rangoon)

Krishna R. PONDICHERRY Bengal

Panaji

GOA ANDHRA Andaman Is.

KARNATAKA PRADESH (India)

Bangalore Chennai Port Blair

PONDICHERRY (Madras)

Pondicherry ANDAMAN

Laccadive Is. TAMIL PONDICHERRY &

(India) KERALA NADU NICOBAR

LAKSHADWEEP ISLANDS

0 100 200 mi. Trivandrum Nicobar Is.

SRI LANKA (India)

0 200 400 km (Ceylon)

© 2001 Zoltán Grossman Colombo INDIAN OCEAN

mtn@ igc.org MALDIVES

THE LADIES HAVE FEELINGS, SO . . .

SHALL WE LEAVE IT TO THE EXPERTS?

India lives in several centuries at the same time. Somehow we manage to progress and regress simultaneously. As a nation we age by pushing outward from the middle — adding a few centuries on to either end of our extraordinary c.v. We greaten like the maturing head of a hammerhead shark with eyes looking in diametrically opposite directions. I have no doubt that even here in North America you have heard that Germany is considering changing its immigration laws in order to import Indian software engineers. I have even less doubt that

---

Based on a talk, given as the Third Annual Eqbal Ahmad Lecture, February 15, 2001, at Hampshire College, Amherst, Massachusetts.

you've heard of the Naga Sadhu at the Kumbh Mela who towed the District Commissioner's car with his penis while the Commissioner sat in it solemnly with his wife and children.

As Indian citizens we subsist on a regular diet of caste massacres and nuclear tests, mosque breakings and fashion shows, church burnings and expanding cell phone networks, bonded labor and the digital revolution, female infanticide and the Nasdaq crash, husbands who continue to burn their wives for dowry and our delectable stockpile of Miss Worlds. I don't mean to put a simplistic value judgment on this peculiar form of "progress" by suggesting that Modern is Good and Traditional is Bad — or vice versa. What's hard to reconcile oneself to, both personally and politically, is the schizophrenic nature of it. That applies not just to the ancient/modern conundrum, but to the utter illogic of what appears to be the current national enterprise. In the lane behind my house, every night I walk past road gangs of emaciated laborers digging a trench to lay fiber-optic cables to speed up our digital revolution. In the bitter winter cold, they work by the light of a few candles.

It's as though the people of India have been rounded

up and loaded onto two convoys of trucks (a huge big one and a tiny little one) that have set off resolutely in opposite directions. The tiny convoy is on its way to a glittering destination somewhere near the top of the world. The other convoy just melts into the darkness and disappears. A cursory survey that tallies the caste, class, and religion of who gets to be on which convoy would make a good Lazy Person's Concise Guide to the History of India. For some of us, life in India is like being suspended between two of the trucks, one in each convoy, and being neatly dismembered as they move apart, not bodily, but emotionally and intellectually.

Of *course* India is a microcosm of the world. Of *course* versions of what happens there happen everywhere. Of *course,* if you're willing to look, the parallels are easy to find. The difference in India is only in the scale, the magnitude, and the sheer proximity of the disparity. In India your face is slammed right up against it. To address it, to deal with it, to not deal with it, to try and understand it, to insist on not understanding it, to simply survive it — on a daily, hourly basis — is a fine art in itself. Either an art or a form of insular, inward-looking insanity. Or both.

To be a writer — a supposedly "famous" writer — in a country where three hundred million people are illiterate is a dubious honor. To be a writer in a country that gave the world Mahatma Gandhi, that invented the concept of nonviolent resistance, and then, half a century later, followed that up with nuclear tests is a ferocious burden. (Though no more ferocious a burden, it has to be said, than being a writer in a country that has enough nuclear weapons to destroy the earth several times over.) To be a writer in a country where something akin to an undeclared civil war is being waged on its subjects in the name of "development" is an onerous responsibility. When it comes to writers and writing, I use words like "onerous" and "responsibility" with a heavy heart and not a small degree of sadness.

This is what I'm here to talk to you, to think aloud with you, about. What is the role of writers and artists in society? Do they have a definable role? Can it be fixed, described, characterized in any definite way? Should it be?

Personally, I can think of few things more terrifying than if writers and artists were charged with an immutable charter of duties and responsibilities that they had to live and work by. Imagine if there was this little black book — a sort of Approved Guide to Good Writing — that said: All writers shall be politically conscious and sexually moral, or: All writers should believe in God, globalization, and the joys of family life . . . .

Rule One for a writer, as far as I'm concerned, is There Are No Rules. And Rule Two (since Rule One was made to be broken) is There Are No Excuses for Bad Art. Painters, writers, singers, actors, dancers, filmmakers, musicians are meant to fly, to push at the frontiers, to worry the edges of the human imagination, to conjure beauty from the most unexpected things, to find magic in places where others never thought to look. If you limit the trajectory of their flight, if you weight their wings with society's existing notions of morality and responsibility, if you truss them up with preconceived values, you subvert their endeavor.

A good or great writer may refuse to accept any responsibility or morality that society wishes to impose on her. Yet the best and greatest of them know that if they abuse this hard-won freedom, it can only lead to bad art. There is an intricate web of morality, rigor, and responsibility that art, that writing itself, imposes on a writer. It's singular, it's individual, but nevertheless it's there. At its

5

best, it's an exquisite bond between the artist and the medium. At its acceptable end, it's a sort of sensible co-operation. At its worst, it's a relationship of disrespect and exploitation.

The absence of external rules complicates things. There's a very thin line that separates the strong, true, bright bird of the imagination from the synthetic, noisy bauble. Where is that line? How do you recognize it? How do you know you've crossed it? At the risk of sounding esoteric and arcane, I'm tempted to say that you just know. The fact is that nobody — no reader, no reviewer, agent, publisher, colleague, friend, or enemy — can tell for sure. A writer just has to ask herself that question and answer it as honestly as possible. The thing about this "line" is that once you learn to recognize it, once you see it, it's impossible to ignore. You have no choice but to live with it, to follow it through. You have to bear with all its complexities, contradictions, and demands. And that's not always easy. It doesn't always lead to compliments and standing ovations. It can lead you to the strangest, wildest places. In the midst of a bloody military coup, for instance, you could find yourself fascinated by the mating rituals of a purple sunbird, or the secret life of captive goldfish, or an old aunt's descent into madness. And nobody can say that there isn't truth and art and beauty in that. Or, on the contrary, in the midst of putative peace, you could, like me, be unfortunate enough to stumble on a silent war. The trouble is that once you see it, you can't unsee it. And once you've seen it, keeping quiet, saying nothing, becomes as political an act as speaking out. There's no innocence. Either way, you're accountable.

Today, perhaps more so than in any other era in history, the writer's right to free speech is guarded and defended by the civil societies and state establishments of the most powerful countries in the world. Any overt attempt to silence or muffle a voice is met with furious opposition. The writer is embraced and protected. This is a wonderful thing. The writer, the actor, the musician, the filmmaker — they have become radiant jewels in the crown of modern civilization. The artist, I imagine, is finally as free as he or she will ever be. Never before have so many writers had their books published. (And now, of course, we have the Internet.) Never before have we been more commercially viable. We live and prosper in the heart of the marketplace. True, for every so-called success there are hundreds who "fail." True, there are myriad art forms, both folk and classical, myriad languages, myriad cultural and artistic traditions that are being crushed and cast aside in the stampede to the big bumper sale in Wonderland. Still, there have never been more writers, singers, actors, or painters who have become influential, wealthy superstars. And they, the successful ones, spawn a million imitators, they become the torchbearers, their work becomes the benchmark for what art is, or ought to be.

Nowadays in India the scene is almost farcical. Following the recent commercial success of some Indian authors, Western publishers are desperately prospecting for the next big Indo-Anglian work of fiction. They're doing everything short of interviewing English-speaking Indians for the post of "writer." Ambitious middle-class parents who, a few years ago, would only settle for a future in Engineering, Medicine, or Management for their children, now hopefully send them to creative writing schools. People like myself are constantly petitioned by computer companies, watch manufacturers, even media magnates to endorse their products. A boutique owner in Bombay once asked me if he could "display" my book

Power Politics

The God of Small Things (as if it were an accessory, a brace-let or a pair of earrings) while he filmed me shopping for clothes! Jhumpa Lahiri, the American writer of Indian origin who won the Pulitzer Prize, came to India recently to have a traditional Bengali wedding. The wedding was reported on the front page of national newspapers.

Now where does all this lead us? Is it just harmless nonsense that's best ignored? How does all this ardent wooing affect our art? What kind of lenses does it put in our spectacles? How far does it remove us from the world around us?

There is very real danger that this neoteric seduction can shut us up far more effectively than violence and re-pression ever could. We have free speech. Maybe. But do we have Really Free Speech? If what we have to say doesn't "sell," will we still say it? Can we? Or is every-body looking for Things That Sell to say? Could writers end up playing the role of palace entertainers? Or the subtle twenty-first-century version of court eunuchs at-tending to the pleasures of our incumbent CEOs? You know — naughty, but nice. Risqué perhaps, but not risky.

Arundhati Roy

It has been nearly four years now since my first, and so far only, novel, *The God of Small Things,* was published. In the early days, I used to be described — introduced — as the author of an almost freakishly "successful" (if I may use so vulgar a term) first book. Nowadays I'm introduced as something of a freak myself. I am, apparently, what is known in twenty-first-century vernacular as a "writer-activist." (Like a sofa-bed.)

Why am I called a "writer-activist" and why — even when it's used approvingly, admiringly — does that term make me flinch? I'm called a writer-activist because after writing *The God of Small Things* I wrote three political essays: "The End of Imagination," about India's nuclear tests, "The Greater Common Good," about Big Dams and the "development" debate, and "Power Politics: The Reincarnation of Rumpelstiltskin," about the privatization and corporatization of essential infrastructure like water and electricity. Apart from the building of the temple in Ayodhya, these currently also happen to be the top priorities of the Indian government.

Now, I've been wondering why it should be that the person who wrote *The God of Small Things* is called a writer, and the person who wrote the political essays is called an activist? True, *The God of Small Things* is a work of fiction, but it's no less political than any of my essays. True, the essays are works of nonfiction, but since when did writers forgo the right to write nonfiction?

My thesis — my humble theory, as we say in India — is that I've been saddled with this double-barreled appellation, this awful professional label, not because my work is political, but because in my essays, which are about very contentious issues, I take sides. I take a position. I have a point of view. What's worse, I make it clear that I think it's right and moral to take that position, and what's even worse, I use everything in my power to flagrantly solicit support for that position. Now, for a writer of the twenty-first century, that's considered a pretty uncool, unsophisticated thing to do. It skates uncomfortably close to the territory occupied by political party ideologues — a breed of people that the world has learned (quite rightly) to mistrust. I'm aware of this. I'm all for being circumspect. I'm all for discretion, prudence, tentativeness, subtlety, ambiguity, complexity. I love the unanswered question, the unresolved story, the unclimbed mountain, the tender shard of an incomplete dream. Most of the time.

But is it mandatory for a writer to be ambiguous about everything? Isn't it true that there have been fearful episodes in human history when prudence and discretion would have just been euphemisms for pusillanimity? When caution was actually cowardice? When sophistication was disguised decadence? When circumspection was really a kind of espousal?

Isn't it true, or at least theoretically possible, that there are times in the life of a people or a nation when the political climate demands that we — even the most sophisticated of us — overtly take sides? I believe that such times are upon us. And I believe that in the coming years intellectuals and artists in India will be called upon to take sides.

And this time, unlike the struggle for Independence, we won't have the luxury of fighting a colonizing "enemy." We'll be fighting ourselves.

We will be forced to ask ourselves some very uncomfortable questions about our values and traditions, our vision for the future, our responsibilities as citizens, the legitimacy of our "democratic institutions," the role of the state, the police, the army, the judiciary, and the intellectual community.

Power Politics

Fifty years after independence, India is still struggling with the legacy of colonialism, still flinching from the "cultural insult." As citizens we're still caught up in the business of "disproving" the white world's definition of us. Intellectually and emotionally, we have just begun to grapple with communal and caste politics that threaten to tear our society apart. But in the meanwhile, something new looms on our horizon.

It's not war, it's not genocide, it's not ethnic cleansing, it's not a famine or an epidemic. On the face of it, it's just ordinary, day-to-day business. It lacks the drama, the large-format, epic magnificence of war or genocide or famine. It's dull in comparison. It makes bad TV. It has to do with boring things like jobs, money, water supply, electricity, irrigation. But it also has to do with a process of barbaric dispossession on a scale that has few parallels in history. You may have guessed by now that I'm talking about the modern version of globalization.

What is globalization? Who is it for? What is it going to do to a country like India, in which social inequality has been institutionalized in the caste system for centuries? A country in which seven hundred million people live in rural areas. In which eighty percent of the landholdings are small farms. In which three hundred million people are illiterate.

Is the corporatization and globalization of agriculture, water supply, electricity, and essential commodities going to pull India out of the stagnant morass of poverty, illiteracy, and religious bigotry? Is the dismantling and auctioning off of elaborate public sector infrastructure, developed with public money over the last fifty years, really the way forward? Is globalization going to close the gap between the privileged and the underprivileged, between the upper castes and the lower castes, between the educated and the illiterate? Or is it going to give those who already have a centuries-old head start a friendly helping hand?

Is globalization about "eradication of world poverty," or is it a mutant variety of colonialism, remote controlled and digitally operated? These are huge, contentious questions. The answers vary depending on whether they come from the villages and fields of rural India, from the slums and shantytowns of urban India, from the livingrooms of the burgeoning middle class, or from the boardrooms of the big business houses.

Today India produces more milk, more sugar, more

food grain than ever before. This year government ware-houses are overflowing with forty-two million tons of food grain. That's almost a quarter of the total annual food grain produce. Farmers with too much grain on their hands were driven to despair. In regions that wielded enough political clout, the government went on a buying spree, purchasing more grain than it could possibly store or use. While the grain rots in government warehouses, three hundred and fifty million Indian citizens live below the poverty line and do not have the means to eat a square meal a day. And yet, in March 2000, just before President Clinton's visit to India, the Indian government lifted import restrictions on one thousand four hundred commodities, including milk, grain, sugar, cotton, tea, coffee, and palm oil. This despite the fact that there was a glut of these products in the market.

From April 1 — April Fool's Day — 2001, according to the terms of its agreement with the World Trade Organization (WTO), the Indian government will have to drop its quantitative import restrictions. The Indian market is already flooded with cheap imports. Though India is technically free to export its agricultural produce, in practice most of it cannot be exported because it doesn't meet the first world's "environmental standards." (You don't eat bruised mangoes, or bananas with mosquito bites, or rice with a few weevils in it. Whereas we don't mind the odd mosquito and the occasional weevil.)

Developed countries like the United States, whose hugely subsidized farm industry engages only two to three percent of its total population, are using the WTO to pressure countries like India to drop agricultural subsidies in order to make the market "competitive." Huge, mechanized corporate enterprises working thousands of acres of farmland want to compete with impoverished subsistence farmers who own a couple of acres of land.

In effect, India's rural economy, which supports seven hundred million people, is being garroted. Farmers who produce too much are in distress, farmers who produce too little are in distress, and landless agricultural laborers are out of work as big estates and farms lay off their workers. They're all flocking to the cities in search of employment.

"Trade Not Aid" is the rallying cry of the headmen of the new Global Village headquartered in the shining offices of the WTO. Our British colonizers stepped onto our shores a few centuries ago disguised as traders. We all remember the East India Company. This time around, the colonizer doesn't even need a token white presence in the colonies. The CEOs and their men don't need to go to the trouble of tramping through the tropics, risking malaria, diarrhea, sunstroke, and an early death. They don't have to maintain an army or a police force, or worry about insurrections and mutinies. They can have their colonies and an easy conscience. "Creating a good investment climate" is the new euphemism for third world repression. Besides, the responsibility for implementation rests with the local administration.

In India, in order to clear the way for "development projects," the government is in the process of amending the present Land Acquisition Act (which, ironically, was drafted by the British in the nineteenth century) and making it more draconian than it already is. State governments are preparing to ratify "anti-terrorist" laws so that those who oppose development projects (in Madhya Pradesh, for example) will be counted as terrorists. They can be held without trial for three years. They can have their lands and cattle seized.

Arundhati Roy

Recently, globalization has come in for some criticism. The protests in Seattle and Prague will go down in history. Each time the WTO or the World Economic Forum wants to have a meeting, ministers have to barricade themselves with thousands of heavily armed police. Still, all its admirers, from Bill Clinton, Kofi Annan, and A.B. Vajpayee (the Indian prime minister) to the cheering brokers in the stalls, continue to say the same lofty things. If we have the right institutions of governance in place — effective courts, good laws, honest politicians, participatory democracy, a transparent administration that respects human rights and gives people a say in decisions that affect their lives — then the globalization project will work for the poor, as well. They call this "globalization with a human face."

The point is, if all this were in place, almost *anything* would succeed: socialism, capitalism, you name it. Everything works in Paradise, a Communist State as well as a Military Dictatorship. But in an imperfect world, is it globalization that's going to bring us all this bounty? Is that what's happening in India now that it's on the fast track to the free market? Does any one thing on that lofty list apply to life in India today?

Power Politics

Are state institutions transparent? Have people had a say, have they even been informed — let alone consulted — about decisions that vitally affect their lives? And are Mr. Clinton (or now Mr. Bush) and Prime Minister Vajpayee doing everything in their power to see that the "right institutions of governance" are in place? Or are they involved in exactly the opposite enterprise? Do they mean something else altogether when they talk of the "right institutions of governance"?

On October 18, 2000, in one of the most extraordinary legal decisions in post-independence India, the Supreme Court permitted the construction of the Sardar Sarovar Dam on the Narmada river to proceed. The court did this despite indisputable evidence placed before it that the Sardar Sarovar Project did not have the mandatory environmental clearance from the central government. Despite the fact that no comprehensive studies have ever been done on the social and ecological impact of the dam. Despite the fact that in the last fifteen years not one single village has been resettled according to the project's own guidelines, and that there was no possibility of rehabilitating the four hundred thousand people who would be displaced by the project. In effect,

19

the Supreme Court has virtually endorsed the violation of human rights to life and livelihood.

Big Dams in India have displaced not hundreds, not thousands, but millions — more than thirty million people in the last fifty years. Almost half of them are Dalit and Adivasi, the poorest of the poor. Yet India is the only country in the world that refused permission to the World Commission on Dams to hold a public hearing. The government in Gujarat, the state in which the Sardar Sarovar Dam is being built, threatened members of the commission with arrest. The World Commission on Dams report was released by Nelson Mandela in November 2000. In February 2001, the Indian government formally rejected the report. Does this sound like a transparent, accountable, participatory democracy?

Recently the Supreme Court ordered the closure of seventy-seven thousand "polluting and nonconforming" industrial units in Delhi. The order could put five hundred thousand people out of work. What are these "industrial units"? Who are these people? They're the millions who have migrated from their villages, some voluntarily, others involuntarily, in search of work. They're the people who aren't supposed to exist, the "noncitizens" who survive in the folds and wrinkles, the cracks and fissures, of the "official" city. They exist just outside the net of the "official" urban infrastructure.

Close to forty percent of Delhi's population of twelve million — about five million people — live in slums and unauthorized colonies. Most of them are not serviced by municipal services — no electricity, no water, no sewage systems. About fifty thousand people are homeless and sleep on the streets. The "noncitizens" are employed in what economists rather stuffily call the "informal sector," the fragile but vibrant parallel economy. That both shocks and delights the imagination. They work as hawkers, rickshaw pullers, garbage recyclers, car battery rechargers, street tailors, transistor knob makers, buttonhole stitchers, paper bag makers, dyers, printers, barbers. These are the "industrial units" that have been targeted as nonconforming by the Supreme Court. (Fortunately I haven't heard *that* knock on my door yet, though I'm as nonconforming a unit as the rest of them.)

The trains that leave Delhi these days carry thousands of people who simply cannot survive in the city. They're returning to the villages they fled in the first place. Millions of others, because they're "illegal," have become easy meat for the rapacious, bribe-seeking police and predatory government officials. They haven't yet been driven out of the city but now must live in perpetual fear and anticipation of that happening.

In India the times are full of talk of the "free market," reforms, deregulation, and the dismantling of the "license raj" — all in the name of encouraging entrepreneurship and discouraging corruption. Yet when the state, supported by the judiciary, curbs freedom and obliterates a flourishing market, when it breaks the backs of numerous imaginative, resourceful, small-scale entrepreneurs, and delivers millions of others as fodder to the doorstep of the corruption industry, few comment on the irony.

No doubt it's true that the informal sector is polluting and, according to a colonial understanding of urban land use, "nonconforming." But then we don't live in a clean, perfect world. What about the fact that sixty-seven percent of Delhi's pollution comes from motor vehicles? Is it conceivable that the Supreme Court will come up with an act that bans private cars? The courts and the government have shown no great enthusiasm for closing down big factories run by major industrialists that have polluted rivers, denuded forests, depleted and poisoned ground water, and destroyed the livelihoods of hundreds of thousands of people who depend on these resources for a living. The Grasim factory in Kerala, the Orient Paper Mill in Madhya Pradesh, the "sunrise belt" industries in Gujarat. The uranium mines in Jadugoda, the aluminum plants in Orissa. And hundreds of others.

This is our in-house version of first world bullying in the global warming debate: i.e., We pollute, you pay.

In circumstances like these, the term "writer-activist" as a professional description of what I do makes me flinch doubly. First, because it is strategically positioned to diminish both writers and activists. It seeks to reduce the scope, the range, the sweep of what a writer is and can be. It suggests somehow that the writer by definition is too effete a being to come up with the clarity, the explicitness, the reasoning, the passion, the grit, the audacity, and, if necessary, the vulgarity to publicly take a political position. And, conversely, it suggests that the activist occupies the coarser, cruder end of the intellectual spectrum. That the activist is by profession a "position-taker" and therefore lacks complexity and intellectual sophistication, and is instead fueled by a crude, simple-minded, one-sided understanding of things. But the more fundamental problem I have with the term is that professionalizing the whole business of protest, putting a label on it, has the effect of containing the problem and suggesting that it's up to the professionals — activists and writer-activists — to deal with.

The fact is that what's happening in India today is not a *problem,* and the issues that some of us are raising are not *causes.* They are huge political and social upheavals that are convulsing the nation. One is not involved by virtue of being a writer or activist. One is involved because one is a human being. Writing about it just happens to be the most effective thing I can do. I think it's vital to de-professionalize the public debate on matters that vitally affect the lives of ordinary people. It's time to snatch our futures back from the "experts." Time to ask, in ordinary language, the public question and to demand, in ordinary language, the public answer.

Frankly, however trenchantly, however angrily, however combatively one puts forward one's case, at the end of the day, I'm only a citizen, one of many, who is demanding public information, asking for a public explanation. I have no axe to grind. I have no professional stakes to protect. I'm prepared to be persuaded. I'm prepared to change my mind. But instead of an argument, or an explanation, or a disputing of facts, one gets insults, invective, legal threats, and the Expert's Anthem: "You're too emotional. You don't understand, and it's too complicated to explain." The subtext, of course, is: Don't worry your little head about it. Go and play with your toys. Leave the real world to us.

It's the old Brahminical instinct. Colonize knowledge, build four walls around it, and use it to your advantage. The Manusmriti, the Vedic Hindu code of conduct, says that if a Dalit overhears a *shloka* or any part of a sacred text, he must have molten lead poured into his ear. It isn't a coincidence that while India is poised to take its place at the forefront of the Information Revolution, three hundred million of its citizens are illiterate. (It would be interesting, as an exercise, to find out how many "experts" — scholars, professionals, consultants — in India are actually Brahmins and upper castes.)

If you're one of the lucky people with a berth booked on the small convoy, then Leaving it to the Experts is, or can be, a mutually beneficial proposition for both the expert and yourself. It's a convenient way of shrugging off your own role in the circuitry. And it creates a huge professional market for all kinds of "expertise." There's a whole ugly universe waiting to be explored there. This is not at all to suggest that all consultants are racketeers or that expertise is unnecessary, but you've heard the saying — There's a lot of money in poverty. There are plenty of ethical questions to be asked of those who make a professional living off their expertise in poverty and despair.

For instance, at what point does a scholar stop being a scholar and become a parasite who feeds off despair and dispossession? Does the source of your funding compromise your scholarship? We know, after all, that World Bank studies are among the most quoted studies in the world. Is the World Bank a dispassionate observer of the global situation? Are the studies it funds entirely devoid of self-interest?

Take, for example, the international dam industry. It's worth thirty-two to forty-six billion U.S. dollars a year. It's bursting with experts and consultants. Given the number of studies, reports, books, PhDs, grants, loans, consultancies, EIAs — it's odd, wouldn't you say,

that there is no really reliable estimate of how many people have been displaced by Big Dams in India? That
there is no estimate for exactly what the contribution of
Big Dams has been to overall food production in India?
That there hasn't been an official audit, a comprehensive,
honest, thoughtful, post-project evaluation of a single
Big Dam to see whether or not it has achieved what it set
out to achieve? Whether or not the costs were justified,
or even what the costs actually were?

What *are* the experts up to?

If you manage to ignore the invective, shut out the
din of the Expert's Anthem, and keep your eye on the
ball, you'll find that a lot of dubious politics lurks inside
the stables of "expertise." Probe further, and it all pre-
cipitates in a bilious rush of abuse, intimidation, and
blind anger. The intellectual equivalent of a police baton
charge. The advantage of provoking this kind of uncon-
strained, spontaneous rage is that it allows you to get a
good look at the instincts of some of these normally cau-
tious, supposedly "neutral" people, the pillars of democracy — judges, planners, academics. It becomes very
clear that it's not really a question of experts versus
laypersons or of knowledge versus ignorance. It's the

pitting of one value system against another, one kind of political instinct against another. It's interesting to watch so many supposedly "rational" people turn into irrational, instinctive political beings. To see how they find reasons to support their views, and how, if those reasons are argued away, they continue to cling to their views anyway. Perhaps for this alone, provocation is important. In a crisis, it helps to clarify who's on which side.

A wonderful illustration of this is the Supreme Court's reaction to my essay "The Greater Common Good," which was published in May 1999. In July and August of that year, the monsoon waters rose in the Narmada and submerged villages. While villagers stood in their homes for days together in chest-deep water to protest against the dam, while their crops were submerged, and while the NBA — Narmada Bachao Andolan, the people's movement in the Narmada valley — pointed out (citing specific instances) that government officials had committed perjury by signing false affidavits claiming that resettlement had been carried out when it hadn't, the three-judge bench in the Supreme Court met over three sessions. The only subject they discussed was whether or not the dignity of the court had been undermined. To assist them in their deliberations, they appointed what is called an *amicus curiae* (friend of the court) to advise them about whether or not they should initiate criminal proceedings against the NBA and me for contempt of court. The thing to keep in mind is that, while the NBA was the petitioner, I was (and hopefully still am) an independent citizen. I wasn't present in court, but I was told that the three-judge bench ranted and raved and referred to me as "that woman." (I began to think of myself as the hooker who won the Booker.)

On October 15, 1999, they issued an elaborate order. Here's an extract:

> ... Judicial process and institution cannot be permitted to be scandalised or subjected to contumacious violation in such a blatant manner in which it has been done by her [Arundhati Roy] ... vicious stultification and vulgar debunking cannot be permitted to pollute the stream of justice ... we are unhappy at the way in which the leaders of NBA and Ms. Arundhati Roy have attempted to undermine the dignity of the Court. We expected better behaviour from them ... After giving this matter thoughtful consideration ... we are not inclined to initiate contempt proceedings against the petitioners, its leaders or Arundhati Roy

. . . . after the 22nd of July 1999 . . . nothing has come to our notice which may show that Ms. Arundhati Roy has continued with the objectionable writings insofar as the judiciary is concerned. She may have by now realised her mistake . . .

What's dissent without a few good insults?

Anyway, eventually, as you can see, they let me off. And I continued with my Objectionable Writings. I hope in the course of this lecture I've managed to inspire at least some of the students in this audience to embark on careers as Vicious Stultificators and Vulgar Debunkers. We could do with a few more of those.

On the whole, in India, the prognosis is — to put it mildly — Not Good. And yet one cannot help but marvel at the fantastic range and depth and wisdom of the hundreds of people's resistance movements all over the country. They're being beaten down, but they simply refuse to lie down and die.

Their political ideologies and battle strategies span the range. We have the maverick Malayali professor who petitions the president every day against the communalization of history texts, Sunderlal Bahugana, who risks his life on indefinite hunger strikes protesting the Tehri

Power Politics

Dam, the Adivasis in Jadugoda protesting uranium mining on their lands, the Koel Karo Sanghathan resisting a mega-dam project in Jharkhand, the awe-inspiring Chattisgarh Mukti Morcha, the relentlessly dogged Mazdoor Kisan Shakti Sangathan, the Beej Bachao Andolan in Tehri-Garhwal fighting to save biodiversity of seeds, and of course, the Narmada Bachao Andolan, the people's movement in the Narmada valley.

India's redemption lies in the inherent anarchy and factiousness of its people, and in the legendary inefficiency of the Indian state. Even our heel-clicking, boot-stamping Hindu fascists are undisciplined to the point of being chaotic. They can't bring themselves to agree with each other for more than five minutes at a time. Corporatizing India is like trying to impose an iron grid on a heaving ocean and forcing it to behave.

My guess is that India will not behave. It cannot. It's too old and too clever to be made to jump through the hoops all over again. It's too diverse, too grand, too feral, and — eventually, I hope — too democratic to be lobotomized into believing in one single idea, which is, ultimately, what globalization really is: Life Is Profit.

What is happening to the world lies, at the moment, just outside the realm of common human understanding. It is the writers, the poets, the artists, the singers, the filmmakers who can make the connections, who can find ways of bringing it into the realm of common understanding. Who can translate cash-flow charts and scintillating boardroom speeches into real stories about real people with real lives. Stories about what it's like to lose your home, your land, your job, your dignity, your past, and your future to an invisible force. To someone or something you can't see. You can't hate. You can't even imagine.

It's a new space that's been offered to us today. A new kind of challenge. It offers opportunities for a new kind of art. An art which can make the impalpable palpable, make the intangible tangible, and the invisible visible. An art which can draw out the incorporeal adversary and make it real. Bring it to book.

Cynics say that real life is a choice between the failed revolution and the shabby deal. I don't know . . . maybe they're right. But even they should know that there's no limit to just how shabby that shabby deal can be. What we need to search for and find, what we need to hone and perfect into a magnificent, shining thing, is a new kind of politics. Not the politics of governance, but the politics of resistance. The politics of opposition. The politics of forcing accountability. The politics of slowing things down. The politics of joining hands across the world and preventing certain destruction. In the present circumstances, I'd say that the only thing worth globalizing is dissent. It's India's best export.

POWER POLITICS

THE REINCARNATION
OF RUMPELSTILTSKIN

Remember him? The gnome who could turn straw into gold? Well, he's back now, but you wouldn't recognize him. To begin with, he's not an individual gnome anymore. I'm not sure how best to describe him. Let's just say he's metamorphosed into an accretion, a cabal, an assemblage, a malevolent, incorporeal, transnational multi-gnome. Rumpelstiltskin is a notion (gnotion), a piece of deviant, insidious, white logic that will eventually self-annihilate. But for now, he's more than okay. He's cock of the walk. King of All That Really Counts (Cash). He's decimated the competition, killed all the other kings, the other kinds of kings. He's persuaded us that he's all we have left. Our only salvation.

Arundhati Roy

What kind of potentate is Rumpelstiltskin? Powerful, pitiless, and armed to the teeth. He's a kind of king the world has never known before. His realm is raw capital, his conquests emerging markets, his prayers profits, his borders limitless, his weapons nuclear. To even try and imagine him, to hold the whole of him in your field of vision, is to situate yourself at the very edge of sanity, to offer yourself up for ridicule. King Rumpel reveals only part of himself at a time. He has a bank account heart. He has television eyes and a newspaper nose in which you see only what he wants you to see and read only what he wants you to read. (See what I mean about the edge of sanity?) There's more: a Surround Sound stereo mouth that amplifies his voice and filters out the sound of the rest of the world, so that you can't hear it even when it's shouting (or starving, or dying), and King Rumpel is only whispering, rolling his R's in his North American way.

Listen carefully. This is most of the rest of his story. (It hasn't ended yet, but it will. It must.) It ranges across seas and continents, sometimes majestic and universal, sometimes confining and local. Now and then I'll peg it down with disparate bits of history and geography that could mar the gentle art of storytelling. So please bear with me.

In March this year (2000 A.D.), the President of the United States (H.E., the most exalted plenipotentiary of Rumpeldom) visited India. He brought his own bed, the feather pillow he hugs at night, and a merry band of businessmen. He was courted and fawned over by the genuflecting representatives of this ancient civilization with a fervor that can only be described as indecent. Whole cities were superficially spruced up. The poor were herded away, hidden from the presidential gaze. Streets were soaped and scrubbed and festooned with balloons and welcome banners. In Delhi's dirty sky, vindicated nuclear hawks banked and whistled: *Dekho ji dekho!* Bill is here because we have the Bomb.

Those Indian citizens with even a modicum of self-respect were so ashamed they stayed in bed for days. Some of us had puzzled furrows on our brows. Since everybody behaved like a craven, happy slave when Master visited, we wondered why we hadn't gone the whole distance. Why hadn't we just crawled under Master's nuclear umbrella in the first place? Then we could spend our pocket money on other things (instead of bombs) and still be all safe and slavey. No?

Just before The Visit, the Government of India lifted import restrictions on fourteen hundred commodities, including milk, grain, sugar, and cotton (even though there was a glut of sugar and cotton in the market, even though forty-two million tons of grain were rotting in government storehouses). During The Visit, contracts worth about three (some say four) billion U.S. dollars were signed.

For reasons of my own, I was particularly interested in a Memorandum of Intent signed by the Ogden Energy Group, a company that specializes in operating garbage incinerators in the United States, and S. Kumars, an Indian textile company that manufactures what it calls "suiting blends."

Now what might garbage incineration and suiting blends possibly have in common? Suit-incineration? Guess again. Garbage-blends? Nope. A big hydroelectric dam on the river Narmada in central India. Neither Ogden nor S. Kumars has ever built or operated a large dam before.

The four-hundred-megawatt Shri Maheshwar Hydel

Power Politics

Project being promoted by S. Kumars is part of the Narmada Valley Development Project, which boasts of being the most ambitious river valley project in the world. It envisages building three thousand and two hundred dams (thirty big dams, one hundred and thirty-five medium dams, and the rest small) that will reconstitute the Narmada and her forty-one tributaries into a series of step reservoirs. It will alter the ecology of an entire river basin, affect the lives of about twenty-five million people who live in the valley, and submerge four thousand square kilometers of old-growth, deciduous forest, hundreds of temples, as well as archaeological sites dating back to the Lower Paleolithic Age.

The dams that have been built on the river so far are all government projects. The Maheshwar Dam is slated to be India's first major private hydel power project.

What is interesting about this is not only that it's part of the most bitterly opposed river valley project in India, but also that it is a strand in the skein of a mammoth global enterprise. Understanding what is happening in Maheshwar, decoding the nature of the deals that are being struck between two of the world's great democracies, will go a long way toward gaining a rudimentary grasp of what is being done to us, while we, poor fools, stand by and clap and cheer and hasten things along. (When I say "us," I mean people, human beings. Not countries, not governments.)

Personally, I took the first step toward arriving at this understanding when, over a few days in March this year (2000 A.D.), I lived through a writer's bad dream. I witnessed the ritualistic slaughter of language as I know and understand it. Let me explain.

On the very days that President Clinton was in India, in far away Holland, the World Water Forum was convened. Four thousand five hundred bankers, businessmen, government ministers, policy writers, engineers, economists — and, in order to pretend that the "other side" was also represented, a handful of activists, indigenous dance troupes, impoverished street theater groups, and half a dozen young girls dressed as inflatable silver faucets — gathered at The Hague to discuss the future of the world's water. Every speech was generously peppered with phrases like "women's empowerment," "people's participation," and "deepening democracy." Yet it turned out that the whole purpose of the forum was to press for the privatization of the world's water.

Power Politics

There was pious talk of having access to drinking water declared a Basic Human Right. How would this be implemented, you might ask. Simple. By putting a market value on water. By selling it at its "true price." (It's common knowledge that water is becoming a scarce resource. One billion people in the world have no access to safe drinking water.) The "market" decrees that the scarcer something is, the more expensive it becomes. But there is a difference between valuing water and putting a market value on water. No one values water more than a village woman who has to walk miles to fetch it. No one values it less than urban folk who pay for it to flow endlessly at the turn of a tap.

So the talk of connecting human rights to a "true price" was more than a little baffling. At first I didn't quite get their drift. Did they believe in human rights for the rich, that only the rich are human, or that all humans are rich? But I see it now. A shiny, climate-controlled human rights supermarket with a clearance sale on Christmas Day.

One marrowy American panelist put it rather nicely: "God gave us the rivers," he drawled, "but he didn't put in the delivery systems. That's why we need private enterprise." No doubt with a little Structural Adjustment to the rest of the things God gave us, we could all live in a simpler world. (If all the seas were one sea, what a big sea it would be . . . Evian could own the water, Rand the earth, Enron the air. Old Rumpelstiltskin could be the handsomely paid supreme CEO.)

When all the rivers and valleys and forests and hills of the world have been priced, packaged, bar-coded, and stacked in the local supermarket, when all the hay and coal and earth and wood and water have been turned to gold, what then shall we do with all the gold? Make nuclear bombs to obliterate what's left of the ravaged landscapes and the notional nations in our ruined world?

As a writer, one spends a lifetime journeying into the heart of language, trying to minimize, if not eliminate, the distance between language and thought. "Language is the skin on my thought," I remember saying to someone who once asked what language meant to me. At The Hague I stumbled on a denomination, a sub-world, whose life's endeavor was entirely the opposite of mine. For them the whole purpose of language is to mask intent. They earn their abundant livings by converting bar graphs that plot their companies' profits into consummately written, politically exemplary, socially just policy documents that are impossible to implement and designed to remain forever on paper, secret even (especially) from the people they're written for. They breed and prosper in the space that lies between what they say and what they sell. What they're lobbying for is not simply the privatization of natural resources and essential infrastructure, but the privatization of policy making itself. Dam builders want to control public water policies. Power utility companies want to draft power policies and financial institutions want to supervise government disinvestment.

Let's begin at the beginning. What does privatization really mean? Essentially, it is the transfer of productive public assets from the state to private companies. Productive assets include natural resources. Earth, forest, water, air. These are assets that the state holds in trust for the people it represents. In a country like India, seventy percent of the population lives in rural areas. That's seven hundred million people. Their lives depend directly on access to natural resources. To snatch these away and sell them as stock to private companies is a process of barbaric dispossession on a scale that has no parallel in history.

What happens when you "privatize" something as essential to human survival as water? What happens when you commodify water and say that only those who can come up with the cash to pay the "market price" can have it?

In 1999, the government of Bolivia privatized the public water supply system in the city of Cochabamba and signed a forty-year lease with a consortium headed by Bechtel, a giant U.S. engineering firm. The first thing Bechtel did was to raise the price of water. Hundreds of thousands of people simply couldn't afford it any more. Citizens came out on the streets to protest. A transport strike brought the entire city to a standstill. Hugo Banzer, the former Bolivian dictator (then the president), ordered the police to confront the crowds. One person was killed, and many more were injured. The protest continued because people had no options — what's the option to thirst? In April 2000, Banzer declared Martial Law. The protest continued. Eventually Bechtel was forced to flee its offices. Many people expect Bechtel will try to extort a twelve-million-dollar exit payment from the Bolivian government for loss of future profits.

Cochabamba has a population of six hundred thousand people. Think of what would happen in an Indian city. Even a small one.

Rumpelstiltskin thinks big. Today he's stalking mega-game: dams, mines, armaments, power plants, public water supply, telecommunication, the management and dissemination of knowledge, biodiversity, seeds (he wants to own life and the very process of reproduction), and the industrial infrastructure that supports all this. His minions arrive in third world countries masquerading as missionaries come to redeem the wretched. They have a completely different dossier in their briefcases. To understand what they're really saying (selling), you have to teach yourself to unscramble their vernacular.

Recently, Jack Welch, the CEO of General Electric (GE), was on TV in India. "I beg and pray to the Indian government to improve infrastructure," he said, and added touchingly, "Don't do it for GE's sake, do it for yourselves." He went on to say that privatizing the power sector was the only way to bring India's one billion people into the digital network. "You can talk about information and intellectual capital, but without the power to drive it, you will miss the next revolution."

What he meant, of course, was: "You are a market of one billion customers. If you don't buy our equipment, we will miss the next revolution."

Will someone please tell Jack Welch that of his one billion "customers," three hundred million are illiterate and live without even one square meal a day and two hundred million have no access to safe drinking water? Being brought into the "digital framework" is hardly what's uppermost on their minds.

The story behind the story is as follows: there are four corporations that dominate the production of power-generation equipment in the world. GE is one of them. Together, each year they manufacture (and therefore need to sell) equipment that can generate at least twenty thousand megawatts of power. For a variety of reasons, there is little (read: almost zero) additional demand for power equipment in the first world. This leaves these mammoth multinationals with a redundant capacity that they desperately need to offload. India and China are their big target markets because, between these two countries, the demand for power-generating equipment is ten thousand megawatts per year.

The first world needs to sell, the third world needs to

buy — it ought to be a reasonable business proposition. But it isn't. For many years, India has been more or less self-sufficient in power equipment. The Indian public sector company Bharat Heavy Electricals (BHEL) manufactured and even exported world-class power equipment. All that's changed now. Over the years, our own government has starved it of orders, cut off funds for research and development, and more or less edged it out of a dignified existence. Today BHEL is no more than a sweatshop. It is being forced into "joint ventures" (one with GE and one with Siemens) in which its only role is to provide cheap, unskilled labor while they — Siemens and GE — provide the equipment and the technology.

Why? Why does more expensive, imported equipment suit our bureaucrats and politicians better? We all know why. Because graft is factored into the deal. Buying equipment from your local store is just not the same thing. It's not surprising that almost half the officials named in the major corruption scandal that came to be known as the Jain Hawala case were officials from the power sector involved with the selection and purchase of power equipment.

The privatization of power (felicitous phrase!) is at the top of the Indian government's agenda. The United States is the single largest foreign investor in the power sector (which, to some extent, explains The Visit). The argument being advanced (both by the government and by the private sector) in favor of privatization is that over the last fifty years the government has bungled its brief. It has failed to deliver. The State Electricity Boards (SEBs) are insolvent. Inefficiency, corruption, theft, and heavy subsidies have run them into the ground.

In the push for privatization, the customary depiction of the corrupt, oily, third world government official selling his country's interests for personal profit fits perfectly into the scheme of things. The private sector bristles accusingly. The government coyly acknowledges the accusation and pleads its inability to reform itself. In fact, it goes out of its way to exaggerate its own inefficiencies. This is meant to come across as refreshing candor.

In a speech he made just before he died, Minister for Power P.R. Kumaramangalam said that the overall figure of loss and deficit in the power sector was 7.86 billion U.S. dollars. He went on to say that India's transmission and distribution (T&D) losses are between thirty-five and forty percent. Of the remaining sixty percent, according to the minister, billing is restricted to only forty percent. His conclusion: that only about a quarter of the electricity that is produced in India is metered. Official sources say that this is a somewhat exaggerated account. The situation is bad enough. It doesn't need to be exaggerated. According to figures put out by the Power Ministry, the national average T&D losses are twenty-three percent. In 1947, they were 14.39 percent. Even without the minister's hyperbole, this puts India in the same league as countries with the worst T&D losses in the world, like the Dominican Republic, Myanmar, and Bangladesh.

The solution to this malaise, we discover, is not to improve our housekeeping skills, not to try and minimize our losses, not to force the state to be more accountable, but to permit it to abdicate its responsibility altogether and privatize the power sector. Then magic will happen. Economic viability and Swiss-style efficiency will kick in like clockwork.

But there's a subplot missing in this narrative. Over the years, the SEBs have been bankrupted by massive power thefts. Who's stealing the power? Some of it no doubt is stolen by the poor — slum dwellers, people who live in unauthorized colonies on the fringes of big cities. But they don't have the electrical gadgetry to consume the quantum of electricity we're talking about. The big stuff, the megawatt thievery, is orchestrated by the industrial sector in connivance with politicians and government officers.

Consider as an example the State of Madhya Pradesh, in which the Maheshwar Dam is being built. Seven years ago it was a power surplus state. Today it finds itself in an intriguing situation. Industrial demand has declined by thirty percent. Power production has increased from three thousand, eight hundred and thirteen megawatts to four thousand and twenty-five megawatts. And the State Electricity Board is showing a loss of two hundred and fifty-five million U.S. dollars. An inspection drive solved the puzzle. It found that seventy percent of the industrialists in the state steal electricity! The theft adds up to a loss of nearly one hundred and six million dollars. That's forty-one percent of the total deficit. Madhya Pradesh is by no means an unusual example. States like Orissa, Andhra Pradesh, and Delhi have T&D losses of between thirty and fifty percent (way over the national average), which indicates massive power theft.

No one talks very much about this. It's so much nicer to blame the poor. The average economist, planner, or drawing room intellectual will tell you that the SEBs have gone belly up for two reasons: (a) Because "political compulsions" ensure that domestic power tariffs are kept unviably low, and (b) Because subsidies given to the farm sector result in enormous hidden losses.

The first step that a "reformed" privatized power sector is expected to take is to cut agricultural subsidies and put a "realistic" tariff (market value) on power.

What are political compulsions? Why are they considered such a bad thing? Basically, it seems to me, political compulsions is a phrase that describes the fancy footwork that governments have to perform in order to strike a balance between redeeming a sinking economy and serving an impoverished electorate. Striking a balance between what the market demands and what people can afford is — or certainly ought to be — the primary, fundamental responsibility of any democratic government. Privatization seeks to disengage politics from the market. To do that would be to blunt the very last weapon that India's poor still have — their vote.

Once that's gone, elections will become even more of a charade than they already are and democracy will just become the name of a new rock band. The poor will be absent from the negotiating table. They will simply cease to matter.

But the cry has already gone up. The demand to cut subsidies has almost become a blood sport. It's a small world. Bolivia is only a short walk down the road from here.

When it recommends privatizing the power sector, does the government mean that it is going to permit just anybody who wishes to generate power to come in and compete in a free market? Of course not. There's nothing free about the market in the power sector. Reforming the power sector in India means that the concerned state government underwrites preposterously one-sided Power Purchase Agreements with select companies, preferably huge multinationals. Essentially, it is the transfer of assets and infrastructure from bribe-taker to bribe-giver, which involves more bribery than ever. Once the agreements are signed, they are free to produce power at exorbitant rates that no one can afford. Not even, ironically enough, the Indian industrialists who have been rooting for them all along. They, poor chaps, end up like vultures on a carcass that get chased off by a visiting hyena.

The fish bowl of the drive to privatize power, its truly star turn, is the story of Enron, the Houston-based natural gas company. The Enron project was the first private power project in India. The Power Purchase Agreement between Enron and the Congress Party–ruled State Government of Maharashtra for a six hundred and ninety-five megawatt power plant was signed in 1993. The opposition parties, the Hindu nationalist Bharatiya Janata Party (BJP) and the Shiv Sena, set up a howl of *swadeshi* (nationalist) protest and filed legal proceedings against Enron and the state government. They alleged malfeasance and corruption at the highest level. A year later, when state elections were announced, it was the only campaign issue of the BJP–Shiv Sena alliance.

In February 1995, this combine won the elections. True to their word, they "scrapped" the project. In a savage, fiery statement, the opposition leader L.K. Advani attacked the phenomenon he called "loot-through-liberalization." He more or less directly accused the Congress Party government of having taken a thirteen-million-dollar bribe from Enron. Enron had made no secret of the fact that, in order to secure the deal, it had paid out millions of dollars to "educate" the politicians and bureaucrats involved in the deal.

Following the annullment of the contract, the U.S. government began to pressure the Maharashtra government. U.S. Ambassador Frank Wisner made several statements deploring the cancellation. (Soon after he completed his term as ambassador, he joined Enron as a director.) In November 1995, the BJP–Shiv Sena government in Maharashtra announced a "re-negotiation" committee. In May 1996, a minority federal government headed by the BJP was sworn in at New Delhi. It lasted for exactly thirteen days and then resigned before facing a vote of no confidence in parliament. On its last day in office, even as the motion of no confidence was in progress, the cabinet met for a hurried "lunch" and re-ratified the national government's counter-guarantee (which had become void because of the earlier "cancelled" contract with Enron). In August 1996, the government of Maharashtra signed a fresh contract with Enron on terms that would astound the most hard-boiled cynic.

The impugned contract had involved annual payments to Enron of four hundred and thirty million U.S. dollars for Phase I (six hundred and ninety-five megawatts) of the project, with Phase II (two thousand and fifteen megawatts) being optional. The "re-negotiated" Power Purchase Agreement makes Phase II of the project mandatory and legally binds the Maharashtra State Electricity Board (MSEB) to pay Enron a sum of thirty billion U.S. dollars! It constitutes the largest contract ever signed in the history of India.

In India, experts who have studied the project have called it the most massive fraud in the country's history. The project's gross profits work out to between twelve and fourteen billion dollars. The official return on equity is more than thirty percent. That's almost double what Indian law and statutes permit in power projects. In effect, for an increase in installed capacity of eighteen percent, the MSEB has to set aside seventy percent of its revenue to be able to pay Enron. There is, of course, no record of what mathematical formula was used to "re-educate" the new government. Nor any trace of how much trickled up or down or sideways and to whom.

But there's more: in one of the most extraordinary decisions in its not entirely pristine history, in May 1997, the Supreme Court of India refused to entertain an appeal against Enron.

Today, four years later, everything that critics of the project predicted has come true with an eerie vengeance. The power that the Enron plant produces is twice as expensive as its nearest competitor and seven times as expensive as the cheapest electricity available in Maharashtra. In May 2000, the Maharashtra Electricity Regulatory Committee (MERC) ruled that temporarily, until as long as was absolutely necessary, no power should be bought from Enron. It was based on a calculation that it would be cheaper to just pay Enron the mandatory fixed charges for the maintenance and administration of the plant that they are contractually obliged to pay than to actually buy any of its exorbitant power. The fixed charges alone work out to around two hundred and twenty million U.S. dollars a year for Phase I of the project. Phase II will be nearly twice the size.

Two hundred and twenty million dollars a year for the next twenty years.

Meanwhile, industrialists in Maharashtra have begun to generate their own power at a much cheaper rate, with private generators. The demand for power from the industrial sector has begun to decline rapidly. The SEB, strapped for cash, with Enron hanging like an albatross around its neck, will now have no choice but to make private generators illegal. That's the only way that industrialists can be coerced into buying Enron's exorbitantly priced electricity.

According to the MSEB's calculations, from January 2002 onward, even if it were to buy ninety percent of Enron's output, its losses will amount to 1.2 billion U.S. dollars a year.

That's more than sixty percent of India's annual Rural Development budget.

In contravention of the MERC ruling, the MSEB is cutting back production from its own cheaper plants in order to buy electricity from Enron. Hundreds of small industrial units have closed down because they cannot afford such expensive electricity.

In January 2001, the Maharashtra government (the Congress Party is back in power with a new Chief Minister) announced that it did not have the money to pay Enron's bills. On January 31, only five days after the earthquake in the neighboring state of Gujarat, at a time when the country was still reeling from the disaster, the newspapers announced that Enron had decided to invoke the counter-guarantee and that if the government did not come up with the cash, it would have to auction the government properties named as collateral security in the contract.

At the time that this book is going to press, Enron and the government of Maharashtra are locked in a legal battle in the High Court of the State of Maharashtra. But Enron has friends in high places. It was one of the biggest corporate contributors to President George Bush Jr.'s election campaign. President Bush has helped Enron with its global business from as far back as 1998. So the old circus has started up all over again. The former U.S. Ambassador (Richard Celeste this time) publicly chastised the Maharashtra Chief Minister for reneging on payments. U.S. government officials have warned India about vitiating the "investment climate" and running the risk of frightening away future investors. In other words: Allow us to rob you blind, or else we'll go away.

The pressure is on for re-re-negotiation. Who knows, perhaps Phase III is on the anvil.

In business circles, the Enron contract is called "the

sweetheart deal." A euphemism for rape without redress. There are plenty of Enron clones in the pipeline. Indian citizens have a lot to look forward to.

Here's to the "free" market.

Having said all this, there's no doubt that there *is* a power-shortage crisis in India. But there's another, more serious crisis on hand.

Planners in India boast that India consumes twenty times more electricity today than it did fifty years ago. They use it as an index of progress. They omit to mention that seventy percent of rural households still have no electricity. In the poorest states, Bihar, Uttar Pradesh, and Orissa, more than eighty-five percent of the poorest people, mostly Dalit and Adivasi households, have no electricity. What a shameful, shocking record for the world's biggest democracy.

Unless this crisis is acknowledged and honestly addressed, generating "lots and lots of power" (as Mr. Welch put it) will only mean that it will be siphoned off by the rich with their endless appetites. It will require a very imaginative, very radical form of "structural adjustment" to right this.

"Privatization" is presented as being the only alternative to an inefficient, corrupt state. In fact, it's not a choice at all. It's only made to look like one. Essentially, privatization is a mutually profitable business contract between the private (preferably foreign) company or financial institution and the ruling elite of the third world. (One of the fallouts is that even corruption becomes an elitist affair. Your average small-fry government official is in grave danger of losing his or her bit on the side.)

India's politicians have virtually mortgaged their country to the World Bank. Today, India pays back more money in interest and repayment installments than it receives. It is forced to incur new debts in order to repay old ones. In other words, it's exporting capital. Of late, however, institutions like the World Bank and the International Monetary Fund, which have bled the third world all these years, look like benevolent saints compared to the new mutants in the market. These are known as ECAs — Export Credit Agencies. If the World Bank is a colonizing army hamstrung by red tape and bureaucracy, the ECAs are freewheeling, marauding mercenaries.

Basically, ECAs insure private companies operating in foreign countries against commercial and political risks. The device is called an export credit guarantee. It's quite simple, really. No first world private company wants to export capital or goods or services to a politically and/or economically unstable country without insuring itself against unforeseen contingencies. So the private company covers itself with an export credit guarantee. The ECA, in turn, has an agreement with the government of its own country. The government of its own country has an agreement with the government of the importing country. The upshot of this fine imbrication is that if a situation does arise in which the ECA has to pay its client, its own government pays the ECA and recovers its money by adding it to the bilateral debt owed by the importing country. (So the real guarantors are actually, once again, the poorest people in the poorest countries.) Complicated, but cool. And foolproof.

The quadrangular private company–ECA–government–government formation neatly circumvents political accountability. Though they're all actually business associates, flak from noisy, tiresome nongovernmental organizations and activist groups can be diverted and funneled to the ECA, where, like noxious industrial effluent, it lies in cooling ponds before being disposed of.

The attraction of the ECAs (for both governments and private companies) is that they are secretive and don't bother with tedious details like human rights violations and environmental guidelines. (The rare ones that do, like the U.S. Export–Import Bank, are under pressure to change.) It short-circuits lumbering World Bank–style bureaucracy. It makes projects like Big Dams (which involve the displacement and impoverishment of large numbers of people, which in turn is politically risky) that much easier to finance. With an ECA guarantee, "developers" can go ahead and dig and quarry and mine and dam the hell out of people's lives without having to even address, never mind answer, embarrassing questions.

Now, coming back to Maheshwar . . .

In order to place India's first private Big Dam in perspective, I need to briefly set out the short, vulgar history of Big Dams in India in general and on the Narmada in particular.

The international dam industry alone is worth thirty-two to forty-six billion U.S. dollars a year. In the first world, dams are being decommissioned, blown up. That leaves us with another industry threatened with redundancy desperately in search of dumping grounds.

Fortunately (for the industry), most third world countries, India especially, are deeply committed to Big Dams.

India has the third largest number of Big Dams in the world. Three thousand six hundred Indian dams qualify as Big Dams under the ICOLD (International Commission on Large Dams) definition. Six hundred and ninety-five more are under construction. This means that forty percent of all the Big Dams being built in the world are being built in India. For reasons more cynical than honorable, politicians and planners have successfully portrayed Big Dams to an unquestioning public as symbols of nationalism — huge, wet, cement flags. Jawaharlal Nehru's famous speech about Big Dams being "the temples of modern India" has made its way into primary school textbooks in every Indian language. Every schoolchild is taught that Big Dams will deliver the people of India from hunger and poverty.

Will they? Have they?

To merely ask these questions is to invite accusations of sedition, of being anti-national, of being a spy, and, most ludicrous of all, of receiving "foreign funds." The distinguished Home Minister, Mr. Advani, while speaking at the inauguration of construction at the

Sardar Sarovar Dam site on October 31, 2000, said that the three greatest achievements of his government were the nuclear tests in 1998, the war with Pakistan in 1999, and the Supreme Court verdict in favor of the construction of the Sardar Sarovar Dam in 2000. He called it a victory for "developmental nationalism" (a twisted variation of cultural nationalism). For the Home Minister to call a Supreme Court verdict a victory for his government doesn't say much for the Supreme Court.

I have no quarrel with Mr. Advani clubbing together nuclear bombs, Big Dams, and wars. However, calling them "achievements" is sinister. Mr. Advani then went on to make farcical allegations about how those of us who were against the dam were "working at the behest of ... outsiders" and "those who do not wish to see India becoming strong in security and socio-economic development." Unfortunately, this is not imbecilic paranoia. It's a deliberate, dangerous attempt to suppress outrageous facts by whipping up mindless mob frenzy. He did it in the run up to the destruction of the Babri Masjid. He's doing it again. He has given notice that he will stop at nothing. Those who come in his way will be dealt with by any methods he deems necessary.

Nevertheless, there is too much at stake to remain silent. After all, we don't want to be like good middle-class Germans in the 1930s, who drove their children to piano classes and never noticed the concentration camps springing up around them — or do we?

There are questions that must be asked. And answered. There is space here for no more than a brief summary of the costs and benefits of Big Dams. A brief summary is all we need.

Ninety percent of the Big Dams in India are irrigation dams. They are the key, according to planners, of India's "food security."

So how much food do Big Dams produce?

The extraordinary thing is that there is no official government figure for this.

The India Country Study section in the World Commission on Dams Report was prepared by a team of experts — the former secretary of Water Resources, the former director of the Madras Institute of Development Studies, a former secretary of the Central Water Commission, and two members of the faculty of the Indian Institute of Public Administration. One of the chapters in the study deduces that the contribution of large dams to India's food grain produce is less than ten percent. *Less than ten percent!*

Ten percent of the total produce currently works out to twenty million tons. This year, more than double that amount is rotting in government storehouses while at the same time three hundred and fifty million Indian citizens live below the poverty line. The Ministry of Food and Civil Supplies says that ten percent of India's total food grain produce every year is spoiled or eaten by rats. India must be the only country in the world that builds dams, uproots millions of people, and submerges thousands of acres of forest in order to feed rats.

It's hard to believe that things can go so grievously, so perilously wrong. But they have. It's understandable that those who are responsible find it hard to own up to their mistakes, because Big Dams did not start out as a cynical enterprise. They began as a dream. They have ended as grisly nightmare. It's time to wake up.

So much for the benefits of India's Big Dams. Let's take a look at the costs. How many people have been displaced by Big Dams?

Once again, there is no official record.

In fact, there's no record at all. This is unpardonable

on the part of the Indian state. And unpardonable on the part of planners, economists, funding agencies, and the rest of the urban intellectual community who are so quick to rise up in defense of Big Dams.

Last year, just in order to do a sanity check, I extrapolated an average from a study of fifty-four dams done by the Indian Institute of Public Administration. After quartering the average they arrived at, my very conservative estimate of the number of people displaced by Big Dams in India over the last fifty years was thirty-three million people. This was jeered at by some economists and planners as being a preposterously exaggerated figure. India's Secretary for Rural Development put the figure at forty million.

Today, a chapter in the India Country Study says the figure could be as high as fifty-six million people.

That's almost twice the population of Canada. More than three times the population of Australia.

Think about it: fifty-six million people displaced by Big Dams in the last fifty years. And India still does not have a national rehabilitation policy.

When the history of India's miraculous leap to the forefront of the Information Revolution is written, let it be said that fifty-six million Indians (and their children and their children's children) paid for it with everything they ever had. Their homes, their lands, their languages, their histories.

You can see them from your car window when you drive home every night. Try not to look away. Try to meet their eyes. Fifty-six million displaced, impoverished, pulverized people. Almost half of them are Dalit and Adivasi. (There is devastating meaning couched in this figure.)

There's a saying in the villages of the Narmada valley — "You can wake someone who's sleeping. But you can't wake someone who's pretending to be asleep." When it comes to the politics of forced, involuntary displacement, there's a deafening silence in this country. People's eyes glaze over. They behave as though it's just a blip in the democratic process.

The nicer ones say, "Oh, but it's such a pity. People must be resettled." (Where? I want to scream. Where's the land? Has someone invented a Land-Manufacturing Machine?)

The nasties say, "Someone has to pay the price for National Development."

The point is that fifty-six million is more than a blip, folks. It's civil war.

Quite apart from the human costs of Big Dams, there are the staggering environmental costs. More than three million acres of submerged forest, ravaged eco-systems, destroyed rivers, defunct, silted up reservoirs, endangered wildlife, disappearing biodiversity, and twenty-four million acres of agricultural land that is now waterlogged and saline. Today there are more drought-prone and flood-prone areas in India than there were in 1947. Not a single river in the plains has potable water. Remember, two hundred million Indians have no access to safe drinking water.

Planners, when confronted with past mistakes, say sagely, "Yes, it's true that mistakes have been made. But we're on a learning curve." The lives and livelihoods of fifty-six million people and all this environmental may-hem serve only to extend the majestic arc of their learning curve.

Will they ever get off the curve and actually *learn?*

The evidence against Big Dams is mounting alarm-ingly. None of it appears on the balance sheet. There *is* no balance sheet. There has not been an official audit, a comprehensive, post-project evaluation, of a single Big Dam in India to see whether or not it has achieved what it set out to achieve.

This is what is hardest to believe. That the Indian government's unshakable faith in Big Dams is based on nothing. No studies. No system of checks and balances. Nothing at all. And of course, those of us who question it are spies.

Is it unreasonable to call for a moratorium on the construction of Big Dams until past mistakes have been rectified and the millions of uprooted people have been truly recompensed and rehabilitated? It is the only way an industry that has so far been based on lies and false promises can redeem itself.

Of the series of thirty Big Dams proposed on the main stem of the Narmada river, four are mega-dams. Of these, only one — the Bargi Dam — has been completed. Three are under construction.

The Bargi Dam was completed in 1990. It cost ten times more than was budgeted and submerged three times more land than engineers said it would. To save the cost and effort of doing a detailed survey, in order to mark the Full Reservoir Level, the government closed the sluice gates one monsoon and filled the reservoir without warning. Water entered villagers' homes at night. They had to take their children, their cattle, their pots and pans, and flee up the hillside. The Narmada Control Authority had estimated that seventy thousand people from one hundred and one villages would be displaced. Instead, when they filled the reservoir, one hundred and fourteen thousand people from one hundred and sixty-two villages were displaced. In addition, twenty-six government "resettlement colonies" (which consisted of house plots but no agricultural land) were also submerged. Eventually there was no rehabilitation. Some "oustees" got a meager cash compensation. Most got nothing. Some died of starvation. Others moved to slums in Jabalpur, where they work as rickshaw pullers and construction labor.

Today, ten years after it was completed, the Bargi Dam irrigates only as much land as it submerged. Only five percent of the land its planners claimed it would irrigate. The government says it has no money to make the canals. Yet work has begun downstream, on the mammoth Narmada Sagar Dam, which will submerge two hundred and fifty-one villages, on the Maheshwar Dam, and, of course, on the most controversial dam in history, the Sardar Sarovar.

The Sardar Sarovar Dam is currently ninety meters high. Its final projected height is one hundred and thirty-eight meters. It is located in Gujarat, but most of the villages that will be submerged by its gigantic reservoir are in Maharashtra and Madhya Pradesh. The Sardar Sarovar Dam has become the showcase of India's Violation of Human Rights Initiative. It has ripped away the genial mask of Dams-as-Development and revealed its brutish innards.

I have written about Sardar Sarovar extensively in a previous essay ("The Greater Common Good"), so I'll be brief. The Sardar Sarovar Dam will displace close to half a million people. More than half of them do not officially qualify as "project-affected" and are not entitled to rehabilitation. It will submerge thirty-two thousand acres of deciduous forest.

In 1985, before a single study had been done, before anyone had any idea what the human cost or environmental impact of the dam would be, the World Bank sanctioned a four-hundred-and-fifty-million dollar loan for the dam. The Ministry of Environment's conditional clearance (without any studies being done) came in 1987! At no point in the decision-making process were the people to be affected consulted or even informed about the project. In 1993, after a spectacular struggle by the Narmada Bachao Andolan (NBA), the people of the valley forced the bank to withdraw from the project. The Gujarat government decided to go ahead with the project.

In 1994, the NBA filed a petition in the Supreme Court. For six years, the court put a legal injunction on further construction of the dam. On October 18, 2000, in a shocking two-to-one majority judgment, the Supreme Court lifted the injunction. After having seen fit to hold up the construction for six years, the court chastised (using unseemly, insulting language) the people of the Narmada valley for approaching it too late and said that, on these grounds alone, their petition should be dismissed. It permitted construction to continue according to the guidelines laid down by the Narmada Water Disputes Tribunal.

It did this despite the fact that it was aware that the tribunal guidelines have been consistently violated for thirteen years. Despite the fact that none of the conditions of the environment ministry's clearance have been met. Despite the fact that thirteen years have passed and the government hasn't even produced a resettlement plan. Despite the fact that not a single village has been resettled according to the directives of the tribunal. Despite the fact that the Madhya Pradesh government has stated on oath that it has no land to resettle "oustees" (eighty percent of them live in Madhya Pradesh). Despite the fact that since construction began, the Madhya Pradesh government has not given a single acre of agricultural land to displaced families. Despite the fact that the court was fully aware that even families displaced by the dam at its current height have not been rehabilitated.

In other words, the Supreme Court has actually ordered and sanctioned the violation of the Narmada Water Disputes Tribunal Award.

"But this is the problem with the government," Mr. and Mrs. Well-Meaning say. "It's so inefficient. These things wouldn't happen with a private company. Things like resettlement and rehabilitation of poor people will be so much better managed."

The Maheshwar experience teaches you otherwise.

In a private project, the only things that are better managed are the corruption, the lies, and the swiftness and brutality of repression. And, of course, the escalating costs.

In 1994, the project cost of the Maheshwar Dam was estimated at ninety-nine million U.S. dollars. In 1996, following the contract with S. Kumars, it rose to three hundred and thirty-three million dollars. Today it stands at four hundred and sixty-seven million. Initially, eighty percent of this money was to be raised from foreign investors. There has been a procession of them — Pacgen of the United States and Bayernwerk, VEW, Siemens, and the HypoVereinsbank of Germany. And now, the latest in the line of ardent suitors, Ogden of the United States.

According to the NBA's calculations, the cost of the electricity at the factory gate will be 13.9 cents per kilowatt hour, which is twenty-six times more expensive than existing hydel power in the state, five and a half times more expensive than thermal power, and four times more expensive than power from the central grid. (It's worth mentioning here that Madhya Pradesh today generates one thousand, five hundred megawatts more power than it can transmit and distribute.)

Though the installed capacity of the Maheshwar project is supposed to be four hundred megawatts, studies using twenty-eight years of actual river flow data show that eighty percent of the electricity will be generated only during the monsoon months, when the river is full. What this means is that most of the supply will be generated when it's least needed.

S. Kumars has no worries on this count. They have Enron as a precedent. They have an escrow clause in their contract, which guarantees them first call on government funds. This means that however much (or however little) electricity they produce, whether anybody buys it or not, for the next thirty-five years they are guaranteed a minimum payment from the government of approximately one hundred and twenty-seven million U.S. dollars a year. This money will be paid to them even before employees of the bankrupt State Electricity Board get their salaries.

What did S. Kumars do to deserve this largesse? It isn't hard to guess.

So who's actually paying for this dam that nobody needs?

According to government surveys, the reservoir of the Maheshwar Dam will submerge sixty-one villages. Thirteen will be wholly submerged; the rest will lose their farmlands. As usual, none of the villagers were informed about the dam or their impending eviction. (Of course, if they go to court now they'll be told it's too late, since construction has already begun.)

The first surveys were done under a ruse that a railway line was being constructed. It was only in 1997, when blasting began at the dam site, that realization dawned on people and the NBA became active in Maheshwar. The agency in charge of the survey is the same one that was in charge of the surveys for the Bargi reservoir. We know what happened there.

People in the submergence zone of the Maheshwar Dam say that the surveys are completely wrong. Some villages marked for submergence are at a higher level than villages that are not counted as project-affected. Since the Maheshwar Dam is located in the broad plains of Nimad, even a small miscalculation in the surveys will lead to huge discrepancies between what is marked for submergence and what is actually submerged. The consequences of these errors will be far worse than what happened at Bargi.

There are other egregious assumptions in the "survey." Annexure Six of the resettlement plan states that there are one hundred and seventy-six trees and thirty-eight wells in all the affected sixty-one villages combined. The villagers point out that in just a single village — Pathrad — there are forty wells and more than four thousand trees.

As with trees and wells, so with people.

There is no accurate estimate of how many people will be affected by the dam. Even the project authorities admit that new surveys must be done. So far they've managed to survey only one out of the sixty-one villages. The number of affected households rose from one hundred and ninety (in the preliminary survey) to three hundred (in the new one).

In circumstances such as these, it's impossible for even the NBA to have an accurate idea of the number of project-affected people. Their rough guess is about fifty thousand. More than half of them are Dalits, Kevats, and Kahars — ancient communities of ferrymen, fisherfolk, sand quarriers, and cultivators of the riverbed. Most of them own no land, but the river sustains them and means more to them than to anyone else. If the dam is built, thousands of them will lose their only source of livelihood. Yet simply because they are landless, they do not qualify as project-affected and will not be eligible for rehabilitation.

Jalud is the first of the sixty-one villages slated for submergence in the reservoir of the dam. As early as 1985, twelve families, mostly Dalit, who had small holdings near the dam site had their land acquired. When they protested, cement was poured into their water pipes, their standing crops were bulldozed, and the police occupied the land by force. All twelve families are now landless and work as wage laborers. The new "private" initiative has made no effort to help them.

According to the environmental clearance from the central government, the people affected by the project ought to have been resettled in 1997. To date, S. Kumars hasn't even managed to produce a list of project-affected people, let alone land on which they are to be resettled. Yet, construction continues. S. Kumars is so well entrenched with the state government that they don't even need to pretend to cover their tracks.

This is how India works.

This is the genesis of the Maheshwar Dam. This is the legacy that the Ogden Energy Group of the United States was so keen to inherit. What they don't realize is that the fight is on. Over the last three years, the struggle against the Maheshwar Dam has grown into a veritable civil disobedience movement, though you wouldn't know it if you read the papers. The mainstream media is hugely dependent on revenue from advertising. S. Kumars sponsors massive advertisements for their blended suitings. After their James Bond campaign with Pierce Brosnan, they've signed India's biggest film star — Hrithik Roshan — as their star campaigner. It's extraordinary how much silent admiration and support a hunk in a blended suit can evoke.

Over the last two years, tens of thousands of villagers have captured the dam site several times and halted construction work. Protests in the region forced two companies, Bayernwerk and VEW of Germany, to withdraw from the project. The German company Siemens remained in the fray (angling for an export credit guarantee from Hermes, the German ECA).

In the summer of 2000, the German Ministry of Economic Co-operation and Development sent in a team of experts headed by Richard Bissell (former chairman of the Inspection Panel of the World Bank) to undertake an independent review of the resettlement and rehabilitation aspects of the project. The report, published on June 15, 2000, was unambiguous that resettlement and rehabilitation of people displaced by the Maheshwar Dam was simply not possible.

At the end of August, Siemens withdrew its application for a Hermes guarantee.

The people of the valley don't get much time to recover between bouts of fighting. In September, S. Kumars was part of the Indian Prime Minister's business entourage when he visited the United States. Desperate to replace Siemens, they were hoping to convert their Memorandum of Understanding with Ogden into a final contract. That, fortunately, didn't happen, and now Ogden has withdrawn from the Maheshwar project.

The only time I have ever felt anything close to what most people would describe as national pride was when I walked one night with four thousand people toward the Maheshwar Dam site, where we knew hundreds of armed policemen were waiting for us. Since the previous evening, people from all over the valley had begun to gather in a village called Sulgaon. They came in tractors, in bullock carts, and on foot. They came prepared to be beaten, humiliated, and taken to prison.

We set out at three in the morning. We walked for three hours — farmers, fisherfolk, sand quarriers, writers, painters, filmmakers, lawyers, journalists. All of India was represented. Urban, rural, touchable, untouchable. This alliance is what gives the movement its raw power, its intellectual rigor, and its phenomenal tenacity. As we crossed fields and forded streams, I remember thinking: This is my land, this is the dream to which the whole of me belongs, this is worth more to me than anything else in the world. We were not just fighting against a dam. We were fighting for a philosophy. For a world view.

We walked in utter silence. Not a throat was cleared. Not a *beedi* lit. We arrived at the dam site at dawn. Though the police were expecting us, they didn't know exactly where we would come from. We captured the dam site. People were beaten, humiliated, and arrested.

I was arrested and pushed into a private car that belonged to S. Kumars. I remember feeling a hot stab of shame — as quick and sharp as my earlier sense of pride. This was my land, too. My feudal land. Where even the police have been privatized. (On the way to the police station, they complained that S. Kumars had given them nothing to eat all day.) That evening, there were so many

arrests, the jail could not contain the people. The administration broke down and abandoned the jail. The people
locked themselves in and demanded answers to their
questions. So far, none have been forthcoming.

~

A Dutch documentary filmmaker recently asked me
a very simple question: What can India teach the world?

A documentary filmmaker needs to see to understand. I thought of three places I could take him to.

First, to a "Call Center College" in Gurgaon, on the
outskirts of Delhi. I thought it would be interesting for a
filmmaker to see how easily an ancient civilization can be
made to abase itself completely. In a Call Center College,
hundreds of young English-speaking Indians are being
groomed to staff the backroom operations of giant
transnational companies. They are trained to answer
telephone queries from the United States and the United
Kingdom (on subjects ranging from a credit card inquiry
to advice about a malfunctioning washing machine or
the availability of cinema tickets). On no account must
the caller know that his or her inquiry is being attended
to by an Indian sitting at a desk on the outskirts of Delhi.

The Call Center Colleges train their students to speak in American and British accents. They have to read foreign papers so they can chitchat about the news or the weather. On duty they have to change their given names. Sushma becomes Susie, Govind becomes Jerry, Advani becomes Andy. (Hi! I'm Andy. Gee, hot day, innit? Shoot, how can I help ya?) Actually it's worse: Sushma becomes Mary. Govind becomes David. Perhaps Advani becomes Ulysses.

Call center workers are paid one-tenth of the salaries of their counterparts abroad. From all accounts, call centers are billed to become a multibillion-dollar industry. Recently the giant Tata industrial group announced its plans to redeploy twenty thousand of its retrenched workers in call centers after a brief "period of training" for the business, such as "picking up [the] American accent and slang." The news report said that the older employees may find it difficult to work at night, a requirement for U.S.–based companies, given the time difference between India and the United States.

The second place I thought I'd take the filmmaker was another kind of training center, a Rashtriya Swayamsevak Sangh (RSS) *shakha,* where the terrible backlash to this enforced abasement is being nurtured and groomed. Where ordinary people march around in khaki shorts and learn that amassing nuclear weapons, religious bigotry, misogyny, homophobia, book burning, and outright hatred are the ways in which to retrieve a nation's lost dignity. Here he might see for himself how the two arms of government work in synergy. How they have evolved and pretty near perfected an extraordinary pincer action — while one arm is busy selling the nation off in chunks, the other, to divert attention, is orchestrating a baying, howling, deranged chorus of cultural nationalism. It would be fascinating to actually see how the inexorable ruthlessness of one process results in the naked, vulgar terrorism perpetrated by the other. They're Siamese twins — Advani and Andy. They share organs. They have the ability to say two entirely contradictory things simultaneously, to hold all positions at all times. There's no separating them.

The third place I thought I'd take him was the Narmada valley. To witness the ferocious, magical, magnificent, tenacious, and above all nonviolent resistance that has grown on the banks of that beautiful river.

What is happening to our world is almost too colossal for human comprehension to contain. But it is a terrible, terrible thing. To contemplate its girth and circumference, to attempt to define it, to try and fight it all at once, is impossible. The only way to combat it is by fighting specific wars in specific ways. A good place to begin would be the Narmada valley.

The borders are open. Come on in. Let's bury Rumpelstiltskin.

ON CITIZENS' RIGHTS TO EXPRESS DISSENT

In February 2001, a criminal petition filed by five advocates was listed before the Supreme Court of India. The petition accused Medha Patkar (leader of the Narmada Bachao Andolan), Prashant Bhushan (legal counsel for the NBA), and Arundhati Roy of committing criminal contempt of court by organizing and participating in a demonstration outside the gates of the Supreme Court to protest the court judgment on the Sardar Sarovar Dam on the Narmada river. Based on the petition, the Supreme Court sent notices to the three accused, ordering them to appear personally in court on April 23, 2001.

The case is still pending in court. The maximum punishment for committing contempt of court in India is six months' imprisonment.

Arundhati Roy

Arundhati Roy did not have a lawyer at her trial. Reproduced here is the text of her affidavit in reply to the criminal charges.

IN THE SUPREME COURT OF INDIA
ORIGINAL JURISDICTION
CONTEMPT PETITION (CR) NO: 2/2001
IN THE MATTER OF:
J.R. PARASHAR & ORS
VERSUS
PRASHANT BHUSHAN & ORS
AFFIDAVIT IN REPLY FILED BY RESPONDENT NO: 3

The gravamen of the charges in the petition against me are contained in the FIR [First Information Report] that the petitioners say they lodged in the Tilak Marg police station on the 14th of December 2000. The FIR is annexed to the main petition and is reproduced verbatim below.

First Information Report dated December 14, 2000

I, Jagdish Prasar, with colleagues Shri Umed Singh and Rajender were going out from Supreme Court at 7.00 p.m and saw that Gate No. C was closed.

Power Politics

We came out from the Supreme Court premises from other path and inquired why the gate is close. The were [we were] surrounded by Prasant Bhusan, Medha Patekar and Arundhanti Roy alongwith their companion and they told Supreme Court your father's property. On this we told them they could not sit on Dharna by closing the gate. The proper place of Dharna is parliament. In the mean time Prastant Bhusan said, "You Jagdish Prasar are the tout of judiciary." Again medha said "*sale ko jaan se maar do*" [kill him]. Arundhanti Roy commanded the crow that Supreme Court of India is the thief and all these are this touts. Kill them, Prasant Bhushan pulled by having caught my haired and said that if you would be seen in the Supreme Court again he would get them killed. But they were shouting inspite of the presence of S.H.O and ACP Bhaskar Tilak marg. We ran away with great with great hardship otherwise their goonda might have done some mischief because of their drunken state. Therefore, it is requested to you that proper action may be taken after registering our complaint in order to save on lives and property. We complainants will be highly obliged.

Sd. Complainants.

The main petition is as shoddily drafted as the FIR. The lies, the looseness, the ludicrousness of the charges displays more contempt for the Apex Court than any of the offenses allegedly committed by Prashant Bhushan, Medha Patkar, and myself. Its contents are patently false and malicious. The police station in Tilak Marg, where the FIR was lodged, has not registered a case. No policeman ever contacted me, there was no police investigation, no attempt to verify the charges, to find out whether the people named in the petition were present at the *dharna,* and whether indeed the incident described in the FIR (on which the entire contempt petition is based) occurred at all.

Under the circumstances, it is distressing that the Supreme Court has thought it fit to entertain this petition and issue notice directing me and the other respondents to appear personally in court on the 23rd of April 2001, and to "continue to attend the Court on all the days thereafter to which the case against you stands and until final orders are passed on the charges against you. WHEREIN FAIL NOT."

For the ordinary working citizen, these enforced court appearances mean that in effect, the punishment for the uncommitted crime has already begun.

The facts relating to the petition are as follows:

Contrary to everything the petition says, insinuates and implies — I am not a leader of the Narmada Bachao Andolan. I am a writer, an independent citizen with independent views who supports and admires the cause of the Andolan. I was not a petitioner in the Public Interest Litigation petition in the case of the Sardar Sarovar Project. I am not an "interested party." Prashant Bhushan is not my lawyer and has never represented me.

Furthermore in all humility I aver that I do not know who the petitioners are. That I never tried to murder anybody, or incite anybody to murder anybody, in broad daylight outside the gates of the Supreme Court in full view of the Delhi police. That I did not raise any slogans against the court. That I did not see Prashant Bhushan pulled anyone by having caught their haired and said that if you would be seen in the Supreme Court again he would get them killed. That I did not see Medha Patkar, leader of India's most prominent nonviolent resistance movement, metamorphose into a mediocre film actor and say *"sale ko jaan se maar do."* (Kill the bastard.) That I did not notice the presence of any *"goondas"* in a

Arundhati Roy

"drunken state." And finally, that my name is spelled wrong.

On the morning of the 13th of December 2000, I learned that people from the Narmada valley had gathered outside the gates of the Supreme Court. When I arrived at the Supreme Court at about 11.30 a.m., gate No. C was already closed. Four to five hundred people were standing outside. Most of them were Adivasi people who, as a consequence of the recent Supreme Court judgment that allowed the construction of the Sardar Sarovar Dam to proceed, will lose their lands and homes this monsoon to the rising waters of the reservoir. They have not been rehabilitated. In a few months they will be destitute and have nowhere to go. These people had traveled all the way from the Narmada valley to personally convey their despair and anguish to the court. To tell the court that, in contravention of its order, no land has been offered to them for rehabilitation and that the reality of the situation in the Narmada valley is very different from the one portrayed in the Supreme Court judgment. They asked the Registrar of the Court for a meeting with the Chief Justice.

A number of representatives of peoples' movements

92

in Delhi, and other supporters of the Andolan like myself, were also there to express their solidarity. I would
like to stress that I did not see Prashant Bhushan, the
main accused in the petition, at the *dharna*. Medha
Patkar, who was there, asked me to speak to the people
for five minutes.

My exact words were: "*Mujhe paanch minute bhi nahi
chahiye aapke saamne apni baat rakhne ke liye. Mein aapke
saath hoon.*" (I do not even need five minutes to tell you
why I'm here. I'm here because I support you.) This is
easy to verify as there were several film and television
crews shooting the event. The villagers had cloth labels
hung around their necks that said, "Project-Affected at
90 Meters" (the current height of the dam). As time went
by and it became clear that the request for a meeting with
the Chief Justice was not going to be granted, people
grew disheartened. Several people (who I don't know or
recognize) made speeches critical of the Court, its inac-
cessibility to common people, and its process. Others
spoke about corruption in the judiciary, about the judges
and how far removed they are from ground realities. I
admit that I made absolutely no attempt to intervene. I
am not a policeman or a public official. As a writer I am

deeply interested in peoples' perceptions of the functioning of one of the most important institutions in this country.

However, I would like to clarify that I have never, either in my writing or in any public forum, cast aspersions on the character or integrity of the judges. I believe that the reflexive instinct of the powerful to protect the powerful is sufficient explanation for the kind of iniquitous judgment as in the case of the Sardar Sarovar Project. I did not raise slogans against the court. I did not, as the petition claims, say "Supreme Court *bika hua hai.*" (The Supreme Court has sold out.) I certainly did not "command the crow that Supreme Court of India is the thief and all these are this touts." (Perhaps the petitioners meant "crowd"?)

I went to the *dharna* because I have been deeply distressed and angered by the Supreme Court's majority — and therefore operative — verdict on the Sardar Sarovar Project. The verdict allowed the project to proceed even though the court was well aware that the Narmada Water Disputes Tribunal had been consistently violated for thirteen years. That not a single village had been resettled according to the directives of the tribunal, and that the

Madhya Pradesh government (which is responsible for eighty percent of the oustees) had given a written affidavit in court stating that it has no land to resettle them. In effect, the Supreme Court ordered the violation of the fundamental rights to life and livelihood of hundreds of thousands of Indian citizens, most of them Dalit and Adivasi.

As a consequence of the Supreme Court judgment, it is these unfortunate citizens who stand to lose their homes, their livelihoods, their gods and their histories. When they came calling on the Supreme Court on the morning of December 13, 2000, they were asking the court to restore their dignity. To accuse them of lowering the dignity of the court suggests that the dignity of the court and the dignity of Indian citizens are incompatible, oppositional, adversarial things. That the dignity of one can only exist at the cost of the other. If this is so, it is a sad and shameful proposition. In his Republic Day speech, President K.R. Narayanan called upon the nation, and specifically the judiciary, to take special care of these fragile communities. He said, "The developmental path we have adopted is hurting them, the marginalized, the Scheduled Castes and Scheduled Tribes, and threatening their very existence."

I believe that the people of the Narmada valley have the constitutional right to protest peacefully against what they consider an unjust and unfair judgment. As for myself, I have every right to participate in any peaceful protest meeting that I choose to. Even outside the gates of the Supreme Court. As a writer I am fully entitled to put forward my views, my reasons and arguments for why I believe that the judgment in the Sardar Sarovar case is flawed and unjust and violates the human rights of Indian citizens. I have the right to use all my skills and abilities, such as they are, and all the facts and figures at my disposal, to persuade people to my point of view.

The petition is a pathetic attempt to target what the petitioners perceive to be the three main fronts of the resistance movement in the Narmada valley. The activist Medha Patkar, leader of the Narmada Bachao Andolan and representative of the people in the valley; the lawyer, Prashant Bhushan, legal counsel for the Narmada Bachao Andolan; and the writer (me), who is seen as one of those who carries the voice of the Andolan to the world outside. It is significant that this is the third time that I, as a writer, have had to face legal harassment connected with my writing.

In July 1999, the three-judge bench in the Supreme Court hearing the public interest petition on the Sardar Sarovar Project took offense at my essay "The Greater Common Good," published in *Outlook* and *Frontline* magazines. While the waters rose in the Narmada, while villagers stood in their homes in chest-deep water for days on end, protesting the court's interim order, the Supreme Court held three hearings in which the main topic they discussed was whether or not the dignity of the court had been violated by my essay. On the 15th of October 1999, without giving me an opportunity to be heard, the court passed an insulting order. Here is an extract:

> . . . Judicial process and institution cannot be permitted to be scandalised or subjected to contumacious violation in such a blatant manner in which it has been done by her [Arundhati Roy] . . . vicious stultification and vulgar debunking cannot be permitted to pollute the stream of justice . . . we are unhappy at the way in which the leaders of NBA and Ms. Arundhati Roy have attempted to undermine the dignity of the Court. We expected better behaviour from them . . .

The order contained a veiled warning to me not to continue with my "objectionable writings."

In 1997, a criminal case for Corrupting Public Morality was filed against me in a district magistrate's court in Kerala for my book *The God of Small Things*. It has been pending for the last four years. I have had to hire criminal lawyers, draft affidavits, and travel all the way to Kerala to appear in court.

And now I have to defend myself on this third, ludicrous charge.

As a writer I wish to state as emphatically as I can that this is a dangerous trend. If the court uses the Contempt of Court law, and allows citizens to abuse its process to intimidate and harass writers, it will have the chilling effect of interfering with a writer's imagination and the creative act itself. This fear of harassment will create a situation in which even before a writer puts pen to paper, she will have to anticipate what the court might think of her work. It will induce a sort of enforced, fearful self-censorship. It would be bad for law, worse for literature and sad for the world of art and beauty.

I have written and published several essays and articles on the Narmada issue and the Supreme Court judgment. None of them was intended to show contempt to the court. However, I have every right to disagree with the Court's views on the subject and to express my disagreement in any publication or forum that I choose to. Regardless of everything the operative Supreme Court judgment on the Sardar Sarovar says, I continue to be opposed to Big Dams. I continue to believe that they are economically unviable, ecologically destructive, and deeply undemocratic. I continue to believe that the judgment disregarded the evidence placed before the court. I continue to write what I believe. Not to do so would undermine the dignity of writers, their art, their very purpose. I need hardly add that I also believe that those who hold the opposite point of view to mine, those who wish to disagree with my views, criticize them, or denounce them, have the same rights to free speech and expression as I do.

I left the *dharna* at about 6 p.m. Until then, contrary to the lurid scenario described in the petitioners' FIR, I can state on oath that no blood was spilled, no mob was drunk, no hair was pulled, no murder attempted. A little *khichdi* was cooked and consumed. No litter was left. There were over a hundred police constables and some senior police officers present. Though I would very much like to, I cannot say in good conscience that I have never set eyes on the petitioners because I don't know who they are or what they look like. They could have been any one of the hundreds of people who were milling around on that day.

But whoever they are, and whatever their motives, for the petitioners to attempt to misuse the Contempt of Court Act and the good offices of the Supreme Court to stifle criticism and stamp out dissent strikes at the very roots of the notion of democracy.

In recent months this court has issued judgments on several major public issues. For instance, the closure of polluting industries in Delhi, the conversion of public transport buses from diesel to CNG [compressed natural gas], and the judgment permitting the construction of the Sardar Sarovar Dam to proceed. All of these have had far-reaching and often unanticipated impacts. They have materially affected, for better or for worse, the lives and livelihoods of millions of Indian citizens. Whatever the justice or injustice of these judgments, whatever their finer legal points, for the court to become intolerant of criticism or expressions of dissent would mark the beginning of the end of democracy.

An "activist" judiciary that intervenes in public matters to provide a corrective to a corrupt, dysfunctional executive surely has to be more, not less accountable. To a society that is already convulsed by political bankruptcy, economic distress, and religious and cultural intolerance, any form of judicial intolerance will come as a crippling blow. If the judiciary removes itself from public scrutiny and accountability, and severs its links with the society that it was set up to serve in the first place, it would mean that yet another pillar of Indian democracy will crumble. A judicial dictatorship is as fearsome a prospect as a military dictatorship or any other form of totalitarian rule.

The Tehelka tapes broadcast recently on a national television network show the repulsive sight of the Presidents of the Bhartiya Janata Party and the Samata Party (both part of the ruling coalition) accepting bribes from spurious arms dealers. Though this ought to have been considered *prima facie* evidence of corruption, the Delhi High Court declined to entertain a petition seeking an enquiry into the defense deals that were referred to in the tapes. The bench took strong exception to the petitioner approaching the court without substantial evidence and even warned the petitioner's counsel that if he failed to substantiate its allegations, the court would impose costs on the petitioner.

On the grounds that judges of the Supreme Court were too busy, the Chief Justice of India refused to allow a sitting judge to head the judicial enquiry into the Tehelka scandal, even though it involves matters of national security and corruption in the highest places.

Yet, when it comes to an absurd, despicable, entirely unsubstantiated petition in which all the three respondents happen to be people who have publicly — though in markedly different ways — questioned the policies of the government and severely criticized a recent judgment of the Supreme Court, the Court displays a disturbing willingness to issue notice.

It indicates a disquieting inclination on the part of the court to silence criticism and muzzle dissent, to harass and intimidate those who disagree with it. By entertaining a petition based on an FIR that even a local police station does not see fit to act upon, the Supreme Court is doing its own reputation and credibility considerable harm.

In conclusion, I wish to reaffirm that as a writer I have the right to state my opinions and beliefs. As a free citizen of India, I have the right to be part of any peaceful *dharna*, demonstration, or protest march. I have the right to criticize any judgment of any court that I believe to be unjust. I have the right to make common cause with those I agree with. I hope that each time I exercise these rights I will not be dragged to court on false charges and forced to explain my actions.

The petitioners have committed civil and criminal defamation. They ought to be investigated and prosecuted for perjury. They ought to be made to pay damages for the time they have wasted of this Apex Court by filing these false charges. Above all they ought to be made to apologize to all those citizens who are patiently awaiting the attention of the Supreme Court in more important matters.

THE ALGEBRA
OF INFINITE JUSTICE

In the aftermath of the unconscionable September 11 suicide attacks on the Pentagon and the World Trade Center, an American newscaster said: "Good and Evil rarely manifest themselves as clearly as they did last Tuesday. People who we don't know massacred people who we do. And they did so with contemptuous glee." Then he broke down and wept.

Here's the rub: America is at war against people it doesn't know (because they don't appear much on TV). Before it has properly identified or even begun to comprehend the nature of its enemy, the U.S. government has, in a rush of publicity and embarrassing rhetoric, cobbled together an "International Coalition Against Terror," mobilized its army, its air force, its navy and its media, and committed them to battle.

The trouble is that once America goes off to war, it can't very well return without having fought one. If it doesn't find its enemy, for the sake of the enraged folks back home, it will have to manufacture one. Once war begins, it will develop a momentum, a logic, and a justification of its own, and we'll lose sight of why it's being fought in the first place.

What we're witnessing here is the spectacle of the world's most powerful country reaching reflexively, angrily, for an old instinct to fight a new kind of war. Suddenly, when it comes to defending itself, America's streamlined warships, its cruise missiles, and F-16 jets look like obsolete, lumbering things. As deterrence, its arsenal of nuclear bombs is no longer worth its weight in scrap. Box cutters, penknives, and cold anger are the weapons with which the wars of the new century will be waged. Anger is the lock pick. It slips through customs unnoticed. Doesn't show up in baggage checks.

Who is America fighting? On September 20, the FBI said that it had doubts about the identities of some of the hijackers. On the same day, President George Bush said he knew exactly who the terrorists were and which governments were supporting them. It sounds as though the

President knows something that the FBI and the American public don't.

In his September 20 address to the U.S. Congress, President George Bush called the enemies of America "enemies of freedom." "Americans are asking, 'why do they hate us?'" he said. "They hate our freedoms — our freedom of religion, our freedom of speech, our freedom to vote and assemble and disagree with each other." People are being asked to make two leaps of faith here. First, to assume that The Enemy is who the U.S. government says it is, even though it has no substantial evidence to support that claim. And second, to assume that The Enemy's motives are what the U.S. government says they are, and there's nothing to support that either.

For strategic, military, and economic reasons, it is vital for the U.S. government to persuade the American public that America's commitment to freedom and democracy and the American Way of Life are under attack. In the current atmosphere of grief, outrage, and anger, it's an easy notion to peddle. However, if that were true, it's reasonable to wonder why the symbols of America's economic and military dominance — the World Trade Center and the Pentagon — were chosen as the targets of the attacks. Why not the Statue of Liberty? Could it be that the stygian anger that led to the attacks has its taproot not in American freedom and democracy, but in the U.S. government's record of commitment to and support for exactly the opposite things — to military and economic terrorism, insurgency, military dictatorship, religious bigotry, and unimaginable genocide (outside America)?

It must be hard for ordinary Americans so recently bereaved to look up at the world with their eyes full of tears and encounter what might appear to them to be indifference. It isn't indifference. It's just augury. An absence of surprise. The tired wisdom of knowing that what goes around eventually comes around. American people ought to know that it is not them, but their government's policies that are so hated. All of us have been moved by the courage and grace shown by America's firefighters, rescue workers, and ordinary office-goers in the days that followed the attacks. American people can't possibly doubt that they themselves, their extraordinary musicians, their writers, their actors, their spectacular athletes, and their cinema, are universally welcomed.

America's grief at what happened has been immense

and immensely public. It would be grotesque to expect it to calibrate or modulate its anguish. However, it will be a pity if, instead of using this as an opportunity to try and understand why September 11 happened, Americans use it as an opportunity to usurp the whole world's sorrow to mourn and avenge only their own. Because then it falls to the rest of us to ask the hard questions and say the harsh things. And for our pains, for our bad timing, we will be disliked, ignored, and perhaps eventually silenced.

The world will probably never know what motivated those particular hijackers who flew planes into those particular American buildings. They were not glory boys. They left no suicide notes, no political messages. No organization has claimed credit for the attacks. All we know is that their belief in what they were doing outstripped the natural human instinct for survival or any desire to be remembered. It's almost as though they could not scale down the enormity of their rage to anything smaller than their deeds. And what they did has blown a hole in the world as we knew it.

In the absence of information, politicians, political commentators, and writers (like myself) will invest the act with their own politics, with their own interpretations.

This speculation, this analysis of the political climate in which the attacks took place, can only be a good thing.

But war is looming large. Whatever remains to be said must be said quickly.

Before America places itself at the helm of the International Coalition Against Terror, before it invites (and coerces) countries to actively participate in its almost godlike mission — called Operation Infinite Justice until it was pointed out that this could be seen as an insult to Muslims, who believe that only Allah can mete out infinite justice, and was renamed Operation Enduring Freedom — it would help if some small clarifications are made. For example, Infinite Justice/Enduring Freedom for whom?

Is this America's War Against Terror in America or against terror in general? What exactly is being avenged here? Is it the tragic loss of almost seven thousand lives, the gutting of fifteen million square feet of office space in Manhattan, the destruction of a section of the Pentagon, the loss of several hundreds of thousands of jobs, the potential bankruptcy of some airline companies, and the crash of the New York Stock Exchange? Or is it more than that?

Power Politics

In 1996, Madeleine Albright, then the U.S. Ambassador to the United Nations, was asked on national television what she felt about the fact that five hundred thousand Iraqi children had died as a result of U.S.-led economic sanctions. She replied that it was "a very hard choice," but that all things considered, "we think the price is worth it." Albright never lost her job for saying this. She continued to travel the world representing the views and aspirations of the U.S. government. More pertinently, the sanctions against Iraq remain in place. Children continue to die.

So here we have it. The equivocating distinction between civilization and savagery, between the "massacre of innocent people" or, if you like, "a clash of civilizations," and "collateral damage." The sophistry and fastidious algebra of Infinite Justice. How many dead Iraqis will it take to make the world a better place? How many dead Afghans for every dead American? How many dead children for every dead man? How many dead mujahideen for each dead investment banker?

As we watch mesmerized, Operation Enduring Freedom unfolds on television monitors across the world. A coalition of the world's superpowers is closing in on Afghanistan, one of the poorest, most ravaged, war-torn countries in the world, whose ruling Taliban government is sheltering Osama bin Laden, the man being held responsible for the September 11 attacks. The only thing in Afghanistan that could possibly count as collateral value is its citizenry. (Among them, half a million maimed orphans. There are accounts of hobbling stampedes that occur when artificial limbs are airdropped into remote, inaccessible villages.)

Afghanistan's economy is in a shambles. In fact, the problem for an invading army is that Afghanistan has no conventional coordinates or signposts to plot on a map — no military bases, no industrial complexes, no water treatment plants. Farms have been turned into mass graves. The countryside is littered with land mines — ten million is the most recent estimate. The American army would first have to clear the mines and build roads in order to take its soldiers in.

Fearing an attack from America, one million citizens have fled from their homes and arrived at the border between Pakistan and Afghanistan. The United Nations estimates that there are 7.5 million Afghan citizens who will need emergency aid. As supplies run out — food and aid agencies have been evacuated — the BBC reports that one of the worst humanitarian disasters of recent times has begun to unfold. Witness the Infinite Justice of the new century. Civilians starving to death while they're waiting to be killed.

In America there has been rough talk of "bombing Afghanistan back to the stone age." Someone please break the news that Afghanistan is already there. And if it's any consolation, America played no small part in helping it on its way. The American people may be a little fuzzy about where exactly Afghanistan is (we hear reports that there's a run on maps of the country), but the U.S. government and Afghanistan are old friends.

In 1979, after the Soviet invasion of Afghanistan, the CIA and Pakistan's ISI (Inter Services Intelligence) launched the CIA's largest covert operation since the Vietnam War. Their purpose was to harness the energy of Afghan resistance to the Soviets and expand it into a holy war, an Islamic jihad, which would turn Muslim countries within the Soviet Union against the Communist regime and eventually destabilize it. When it began, it was meant to be the Soviet Union's Vietnam. It turned out to be much more than that. Over the years, through the ISI, the CIA funded and recruited tens of thousands of radical mujahideen from forty Islamic countries as soldiers for America's proxy war. The rank-and-file of the mujahideen were unaware that their jihad was actually being fought on behalf of Uncle Sam. (The irony is that America was equally unaware that it was financing a future war against itself.)

In 1989, after being bloodied by ten years of relentless conflict, the Russians withdrew, leaving behind a civilization reduced to rubble. Civil war in Afghanistan raged on. The jihad spread to Chechnya, Kosovo, and eventually Kashmir. The CIA continued to pour in money and military equipment, but the overheads had become immense, and more money was needed. The mujahideen ordered farmers to plant opium as a "revolutionary tax." Under the proection of the ISI, hundreds of heroin processing laboratories were set up across Afghanistan. Within two years of the CIA's arrival, the Pakistan Afghanistan borderland had become the biggest producer of heroin in the world, and the single biggest source on American streets. The annual profits, said to be between one hundred and two hundred billion dollars, were ploughed back into training and arming militants.

Power Politics

In 1996, the Taliban — then a marginal sect of dangerous, hard-line fundamentalists — fought its way to power in Afghanistan. It was funded by the ISI, that old cohort of the CIA, and supported by many political parties in Pakistan. The Taliban unleashed a regime of terror. Its first victims were its own people, particularly women. It closed down girls' schools, dismissed women from government jobs, enforced Sharia laws under which women deemed to be "immoral" are stoned to death, and widows guilty of being adulterous are buried alive. Given the Taliban government's human rights track record, it seems unlikely that it will in any way be intimidated or swerved from its purpose by the prospect of war, or the threat to the lives of its civilians.

After all that has happened, can there be anything more ironic than Russia and America joining hands to re-destroy Afghanistan? The question is, can you destroy destruction? Dropping more bombs on Afghanistan will only shuffle the rubble, scramble some old graves, and disturb the dead.

The desolate landscape of Afghanistan was the burial ground of Soviet Communism and the springboard of a unipolar world dominated by America. It made the space for neo-capitalism and corporate globalization, again dominated by America. And now Afghanistan is poised to become the graveyard for the unlikely soldiers who fought and won this war for America.

And what of America's trusted ally? Pakistan, too, has suffered enormously. The U.S. government has not been shy of supporting military dictators who have blocked the idea of democracy from taking root in the country. Before the CIA arrived, there was a small rural market for opium in Pakistan. Between 1979 and 1985, the number of heroin addicts grew from next to nothing to a massive number. Even before September 11, there were millions of Afghan refugees living in tented camps along the border.

Pakistan's economy is crumbling. Sectarian violence, globalization's Structural Adjustment Programs, and drug lords are tearing the country to pieces. Set up to fight the Soviets, the terrorist training centers and madrassas, sown like dragon's teeth across the country, produced fundamentalists with tremendous popular appeal within Pakistan itself. The Taliban, which the Pakistan government has supported, funded, and propped up for years, has material and strategic alliances with Pakistan's own political parties. Now the U.S. government is asking (asking?) Pakistan to garrote the pet it has hand-reared in its backyard for so many years. President Pervez Musharraf, having pledged his support to the U.S., could well find he has something resembling civil war on his hands.

India, thanks in part to its geography, and in part to the vision of its former leaders, has so far been fortunate enough to be left out of this Great Game. Had it been drawn in, it's more than likely that our democracy, such as it is, would not have survived. Today, as some of us watch in horror, the Indian government is furiously gyrating its hips, begging the U.S. to set up its base in India rather than Pakistan.

Having had this ringside view of Pakistan's sordid fate, it isn't just odd, it's unthinkable, that India should want to do this. Any third world country with a fragile economy and a complex social base should know by now that to invite a superpower such as America in (whether it says it's staying or just passing through) would be like inviting a brick to drop through your winsdshield.

In the media blitz that followed September 11, mainstream television stations largely ignored the story of America's involvement with Afghanistan. So, to those unfamiliar with the story, the coverage of the attacks could have been moving, disturbing, and, perhaps to cynics, self-indulgent. However, to those of us who are familiar with Afghanistan's recent history, American TV coverage and the rhetoric of the International Coalition Against Terror is just plain insulting. America's "free press," like its "free market," has a lot to account for.

Operation Enduring Freedom is ostensibly being fought to uphold the American Way of Life. It'll probably end up undermining it completely. It will spawn more anger and more terror across the world. For ordinary people in America, it will mean lives lived in a climate of sickening uncertainty: will my child be safe in school? Will there be nerve gas in the subway? A bomb in the cinema hall? Will my love come home tonight? There have been warnings about the possibility of biological warfare — small pox, bubonic plague, anthrax — the deadly payload of an innocuous crop duster. Being picked off a few at a time may end up being worse than being annihilated all at once by a nuclear bomb.

The U.S. government, and no doubt governments all over the world, will use the climate of war as an excuse to curtail civil liberties, deny free speech, lay off workers, harass ethnic and religious minorities, cut back on public spending, and divert huge amounts of money to the defense industry.

To what purpose? President George Bush can no more "rid the world of evildoers" than he can stock it with saints. It's absurd for the U.S. government to even toy with the notion that it can stamp out terrorism with more violence and oppression. Terrorism is the symptom, not the disease. Terrorism has no country. It's transnational, as global an enterprise as Coke or Pepsi or Nike. At the first sign of trouble, terrorists can pull up stakes and move their "factories" from country to country in search of a better deal. Just like the multinationals.

Terrorism as a phenomenon may never go away. But if it is to be contained, the first step is for America to at least acknowledge that it shares the planet with other nations, with other human beings, who, even if they are not on TV, have loves and griefs and stories and songs and sorrows and, for heavens' sake, rights. Instead, when Donald Rumsfeld, the U.S. Defense Secretary, was asked what he would call a victory in America's new war, he said that if he could convince the world that Americans must be allowed to continue with their way of life, he would consider it a victory.

The September 11 attacks were a monstrous calling card from a world gone horribly wrong. The message may have been written by bin Laden (who knows?) and delivered by his couriers, but it could well have been signed by the ghosts of the victims of America's old wars.

The millions killed in Korea, Vietnam and Cambodia, the seventeen thousand killed when Israel — backed by the United States — invaded Lebanon in 1982, the tens of thousands of Iraqis killed in Operation Desert Storm, the thousands of Palestinians who have died fighting Israel's occupation of the West Bank. And the millions who died, in Yugoslavia, Somalia, Haiti, Chile, Nicaragua, El Salvador, the Dominican Republic, Panama, at the hands of all the terrorists, dictators, and genocidists who the American government supported, trained, bankrolled, and supplied with arms. And this is far from being a comprehensive list.

For a country involved in so much warfare and conflict, the American people have been extremely fortunate. The strikes on September 11 were only the second on American soil in more than a century. The first was

Power Politics

Pearl Harbor. The reprisal for this took a long route, but ended with Hiroshima and Nagasaki. This time the world waits with bated breath for the horrors to come.

Someone recently said that if Osama bin Laden didn't exist, America would have had to invent him. But in a way, America did invent him. He was among the jihadists who moved to Afghanistan in 1979 when the CIA commenced its operations there. Bin Laden has the distinction of being created by the CIA and wanted by the FBI. In the course of a fortnight, he has been promoted from Suspect to Prime Suspect, and then, despite the lack of any real evidence, straight up the charts to being "wanted dead or alive."

From all accounts, it will be impossible to produce evidence (of the sort that would stand scrutiny in a court of law) to link bin Laden to the September 11 attacks. So far, it appears that the most incriminating piece of evidence against him is the fact that he has not condemned them. From what is known about the location of bin Laden and the living conditions where he operates, it's entirely possible that he did not personally plan and carry out the attacks — that he is the inspirational figure, "the CEO of the holding company."

The Taliban's response to U.S. demands for the extradition of bin Laden has been uncharacteristically reasonable: produce the evidence, then we'll hand him over. President Bush's response is that the demand is "non-negotiable."

(While talks are on for the extradition of CEOs — can India put in a side request for the extradition of Warren Anderson of the U.S.A.? He was the Chairman of Union Carbide, responsible for the 1984 Bhopal gas leak, which killed sixteen thousand people. We have collated the necessary evidence. It's all in the files. Could we have him, please?)

But who is Osama bin Laden really?

Let me rephrase that. What is Osama bin Laden?

He's America's family secret. He is the American President's dark doppelganger. The savage twin of all that purports to be beautiful and civilized. He has been sculpted from the spare rib of a world laid to waste by America's foreign policy: its gunboat diplomacy, its nuclear arsenal, its vulgarly stated policy of "full spectrum dominance," its chilling disregard for non-American lives, its barbarous military interventions, its support for despotic and dictatorial regimes, its merciless economic agenda that has munched through the economies of poor countries like a cloud of locusts. Its marauding multinationals, which are taking over the air we breathe, the ground we stand on, the water we drink, the thoughts we think.

Now that the family secret has been spilled, the twins are blurring into one another and gradually becoming interchangeable. Their guns, bombs, money, and drugs have been going around in the loop for a while. (The Stinger missiles that will greet U.S. helicopters were supplied by the CIA. The heroin used by America's drug addicts comes from Afghanistan. The Bush administration recently gave Afghanistan a forty-three million dollar subsidy to its "war on drugs.")

Now they've even begun to borrow each other's rhetoric. Each refers to the other as "the head of the snake." Both invoke God and use the loose millenarian currency of Good and Evil as their terms of reference. Both are engaged in unequivocal political crimes.

Both are dangerously armed — one with the nuclear arsenal of the obscenely powerful, the other with the incandescent, destructive power of the utterly hopeless.

The fireball and the ice pick. The bludgeon and the axe. The important thing to keep in mind is that neither is an acceptable alternative to the other.

President Bush's ultimatum to the people of the world — "Either you are with us or you are with the terrorists" — is a piece of presumptuous arrogance.

It's not a choice that people want to, need to, or should have to make.

WAR IS PEACE

As darkness deepened over Afghanistan on Sunday, October 7, 2001, the U.S. government, backed by the International Coalition Against Terror (the new, amenable surrogate for the United Nations), launched air strikes against Afghanistan. TV channels lingered on computer-animated images of cruise missiles, stealth bombers, Tomahawks, "bunker-busting" missiles, and Mark 82 high drag bombs. All over the world, little boys watched goggle-eyed and stopped clamoring for new video games.

The U.N., reduced now to an ineffective acronym, wasn't even asked to mandate the air strikes. (As Madeleine Albright once said, "We will behave multilaterally when we can and unilaterally when we must.")

The "evidence" against the terrorists was shared amongst friends in the International Coalition. After conferring, they announced that it didn't matter whether or not the "evidence" would stand up in a court of law. Thus, in an instant, were centuries of jurisprudence carelessly trashed.

Nothing can excuse or justify an act of terrorism, whether it is committed by religious fundamentalists, private militias, people's resistance movements — or whether it's dressed up as a war of retribution by a recognised government. The bombing of Afghanistan is not revenge for New York and Washington. It is yet another act of terror against the people of the world. Each innocent person that is killed must be added to, not set off against, the grisly toll of civilians who died in New York and Washington.

People rarely win wars; governments rarely lose them. People get killed. Governments molt and regroup, hydra-headed. They first use flags to shrink-wrap peoples' minds and smother real thought, and then as ceremonial shrouds to bury the willing dead. On both sides, in Afghanistan as well as America, civilians are now hostage to the actions of their own governments. Unknowingly, ordinary people in both countries share a common bond — they have to live with the phenomenon of blind, unpredictable terror. Each batch of bombs that is dropped on Afghanistan is matched by a corresponding escalation of mass hysteria in America about anthrax, more hijackings, and other terrorist acts.

There is no easy way out of the spiralling morass of terror and brutality that confronts the world today. It is time now for the human race to hold still, to delve into its wells of collective wisdom, both ancient and modern. What happened on September 11 changed the world forever. Freedom, progress, wealth, technology, war — these words have taken on new meaning. Governments have to acknowledge this transformation, and approach their new tasks with a modicum of honesty and humility. Unfortunately, up to now, there has been no sign of any introspection from the leaders of the International Coalition. Or the Taliban.

When he announced the air strikes, President George Bush said, "We're a peaceful nation." America's favorite Ambassador, Tony Blair, (who also holds the portfolio of Prime Minister of the U.K.), echoed him: "We're a peaceful people."

So now we know. Pigs are horses. Girls are boys. War is peace.

Speaking at the FBI's headquarters a few days later, President Bush said, "This is the calling of the United States of America, the most free nation in the world, a nation built on fundamental values; that rejects hate, rejects violence, rejects murderers, rejects evil. And we will not tire."

Here is a list of the countries that America has been at war with — and bombed — since World War II: China (1945–1946, 1950–1953), Korea (1950–1953), Guatemala (1954, 1967–1969), Indonesia (1958), Cuba (1959–1960), the Belgian Congo (1964), Peru (1965), Laos (1964–1973), Vietnam (1961–1973), Cambodia (1969–1970), Grenada (1983), Libya (1986), El Salvador (1980s), Nicaragua (1980s), Panama (1989), Iraq (1991–2001), Bosnia (1995), Sudan (1998), Yugoslavia (1999). And now Afghanistan.

Certainly it does not tire — this, the Most Free Nation in the world. What freedoms does it uphold? Within its borders, the freedoms of speech, religion, thought; of artistic expression, food habits, sexual preferences (well, to some extent), and many other exemplary, wonderful things. Outside its borders, the freedom to dominate, humiliate, and subjugate — usually in the service of

America's real religion, the "free market." So when the U.S. government christens a war Operation Infinite Justice, or Operation Enduring Freedom, we in the third world feel more than a tremor of fear. Because we know that Infinite Justice for some means Infinite Injustice for others. And Enduring Freedom for some means Enduring Subjugation for others.

The International Coalition Against Terror is largely a cabal of the richest countries in the world. Between them, they manufacture and sell almost all of the world's weapons. They possess the largest stockpile of weapons of mass destruction — chemical, biological, and nuclear. They have fought the most wars, account for most of the genocide, subjection, ethnic cleansing, and human rights violations in modern history, and have sponsored, armed, and financed untold numbers of dictators and despots. Between them, they have worshipped, almost deified, the cult of violence and war. For all its appalling sins, the Taliban just isn't in the same league.

The Taliban was compounded in the crumbling crucible of rubble, heroin, and land mines in the backwash of the Cold War. Its oldest leaders are in their early forties. Many of them are disfigured and handicapped, missing an eye, an arm, or a leg. They grew up in a society scarred and devastated by war. Between the Soviet Union and America, over twenty years, about forty-five billion dollars worth of arms and ammunition was poured into Afghanistan.

The latest weaponry was the only shard of modernity to intrude upon a thoroughly medieval society. Young boys — many of them orphans — who grew up in those times had guns for toys, never knew the security and comfort of family life, never experienced the company of women. Now, as adults and rulers, the Taliban beat, stone, rape, and brutalize women. They don't seem to know what else to do with them. Years of war has stripped them of gentleness, inured them to kindness and human compassion. They dance to the percussive rhythms of bombs raining down around them. Now they've turned their monstrosity on their own people.

With all due respect to President Bush, the people of the world do not have to choose between the Taliban and the U.S. government. All the beauty of human civilization — our art, our music, our literature — lies beyond these two fundamentalist, ideological poles. There is as little chance that the people of the world can all become middle-class consumers as there is that they will all embrace any one particular religion.

The issue is not about Good versus Evil or Islam versus Christianity as much as it is about space. About how to accommodate diversity, how to contain the impulse toward hegemony — every kind of hegemony: economic, military, linguistic, religious, and cultural. Any ecologist will tell you how dangerous and fragile a monoculture is. A hegemonic world is like having a government without a healthy opposition. It becomes a kind of dictatorship. It's like putting a plastic bag over the world, and preventing it from breathing. Eventually, it will be torn open.

One and a half million Afghan people lost their lives in the twenty years of conflict that preceded this new war.

Afghanistan was reduced to rubble, and now the rubble is being pounded into finer dust. By the second day of the air strikes, U.S. pilots were returning to their bases without dropping their assigned payload of bombs.

As one senior offcial put it, Afghanistan is "not a target-rich environment." At a press briefing at the Pentagon, U.S. Defense Secretary Donald Rumsfeld was asked if America had run out of targets. "First we're going to re-hit targets," he said, "and second, we're not running out of targets, Afghanistan is...." This was greeted with gales of laughter in the briefing room.

By the third day of the strikes, the U.S. Defense Department boasted that it had "achieved air supremacy over Afghanistan" (Did it mean that it had destroyed both, or maybe all sixteen, of Afghanistan's planes?)

On the ground in Afghanistan, the Northern Alliance — the Taliban's old enemy, and therefore the International Coalition's newest friend — is making headway in its push to capture Kabul. (For the archives, let it be said that the Northern Alliance's track record is not very different from the Taliban's. But for now, because it's inconvenient, that little detail is being glossed over.)

The visible, moderate, "acceptable" leader of the Alliance, Ahmed Shah Massoud, was killed in a suicide-bomb attack early in September 2001. The rest of the Nothern Alliance is a brittle confederation of brutal warlords, ex-Communists, and unbending clerics. It is a disparate group divided along ethnic lines, some of whom have tasted power in Afghanistan in the past.

Until the U.S. air strikes, the Northern Alliance controlled about five percent of the geographical area of Afghanistan. Now, with the International Coalition's help and "air cover," it is poised to topple the Taliban. Meanwhile, Taliban soldiers, sensing imminent defeat, have begun to defect to the Alliance. So the fighting forces are busy switching sides and changing uniforms. But in an enterprise as cynical as this one, it seems to matter hardly at all. Love is hate, north is south, peace is war.

Among the global powers, there is talk of "putting in a representative government." Or, on the other hand, of "restoring" the kingdom to Afghanistan's 86-year-old former king, Muhammad Zahir Shah, who has lived in exile in Rome since 1973. That's the way the game goes — support Saddam Hussein, then "take him out"; finance the mujahideen, then bomb them to smithereens; put in Zahir Shah and see if he's going to be a good boy. (Is it possible to "put in" a representative government? Can you place an order for Democracy — with extra cheese and jalapeno peppers?)

Reports have begun to trickle in about civilian casualties, about cities emptying out as Afghan civilians flock to the borders, which have been closed. Main arterial roads have been blown up or sealed off. Those who have experience of working in Afghanistan say that by early November, food convoys will not be able to reach the millions of Afghans (7.5 million according to the U.N.) who run the very real risk of starving to death during the course of this winter. They say that in the days that are left before winter sets in, there can either be a war or an attempt to reach food to the hungry. Not both.

As a gesture of humanitarian support, the U.S. government airdropped thirty-seven thousand packets of emergency rations into Afghanistan. It says it plans to drop more than five hundred thousand packets. That will still only add up to a single meal for half a million people out of the several million in dire need of food. Aid workers have condemned this as a cynical, dangerous, public relations exercise. They say that airdropping food packets is worse than futile. First, because the food will never get to those who really need it. More dangerously, those who run out to retrieve the packets risk being blown up by land mines. A tragic alms race.

Nevertheless, the food packets had a photo-op all to themselves. Their contents were listed in major newspapers. They were vegetarian, we're told, as per Muslim Dietary Law (!) Each yellow packet, decorated with the

Power Politics

American flag, contained rice, peanut butter, bean salad, strawberry jam, crackers, raisins, flat bread, an apple fruit bar, seasoning, matches, a set of plastic cutlery, a napkin, and illustrated user instructions.

After three years of unremitting drought, an air-dropped airline meal in Jalalabad! The level of cultural ineptitude, the failure to understand what months of relentless hunger and grinding poverty really mean, the U.S. government's attempt to use even this abject misery to boost its self-image, beggars description.

Reverse the scenario for a moment. Imagine if the Taliban government was to bomb New York City, saying all the while that its real target was the U.S. government and its policies. And suppose, during breaks between the bombing, the Taliban dropped a few thousand packets containing nan and kababs impaled on an Afghan flag. Would the good people of New York ever find it in themselves to forgive the Afghan government? Even if they were hungry, even if they needed the food, even if they ate it, how would they ever forget the insult, the condescension? Rudi Giuliani, Mayor of New York City, returned a gift of ten million dollars from a Saudi prince because it came with a few words of friendly advice about American policy in the Middle East. Is pride a luxury that only the rich are entitled to?

Far from stamping it out, igniting this kind of rage is what creates terrorism. Hate and retribution don't go back into the box once you've let them out. For every "terrorist" or his "supporter" who is killed, hundreds of innocent people are being killed, too. And for every hundred innocent people killed, there is a good chance that several future terrorists will be created.

Where will it all lead?

Setting aside the rhetoric for a moment, consider the fact that the world has not yet found an acceptable definition of what "terrorism" is. One country's terrorist is too often another's freedom fighter. At the heart of the matter lies the world's deep-seated ambivalence toward violence. Once violence is accepted as a legitimate political instrument, then the morality and political acceptability of terrorists (insurgents or freedom fighters) becomes contentious, bumpy terrain.

The U.S. government itself has funded, armed, and sheltered plenty of rebels and insurgents around the world. The CIA and Pakistan's ISI trained and armed the mujahideen who, in the 1980s, were seen as terrorists by the government in Soviet-occupied Afghanistan, while President Reagan praised them as freedom fighters.

Today, Pakistan — America's ally in this new war — sponsors insurgents who cross the border into Kashmir in India. Pakistan lauds them as freedom fighters, India calls them terrorists. India, for its part, denounces countries that sponsor and abet terrorism, but the Indian army has, in the past, trained separatist Tamil rebels asking for a homeland in Sri Lanka — the LTTE, responsible for countless acts of bloody terrorism.

(Just as the CIA abandoned the mujahideen after they had served its purpose, India abruptly turned its back on the LTTE for a host of political reasons. It was an enraged LTTE suicide bomber who assassinated former Indian Prime Minister Rajiv Gandhi in 1991.)

It is important for governments and politicians to understand that manipulating these huge, raging human feelings for their own narrow purposes may yield instant results, but eventually and inexorably, they have disastrous consequences. Igniting and exploiting religious sentiments for reasons of political expediency is the most dangerous legacy that governments or politicians can bequeath to any people — including their own. People who live in societies ravaged by religious or communal bigotry know that every religious text, from the Bible to the Bhagvad-Gita, can be mined and misinterpreted to justify anything from nuclear war to genocide to corporate globalization.

This is not to suggest that the terrorists who perpetrated the outrage on September 11 should not be hunted down and brought to book. They must be. But is war the best way to track them down? Will burning the haystack find you the needle? Or will it escalate the anger and make the world a living hell for all of us?

At the end of the day, how many people can you spy on, how many bank accounts can you freeze, how many conversations can you eavesdrop on, how many e-mails can you intercept, how many letters can you open, how many phones can you tap? Even before September 11, the CIA had accumulated more information than is humanly possible to process. (Sometimes, too much data can actually hinder intelligence — small wonder the U.S. spy satellites completely missed the preparation that preceded India's nuclear tests in 1998.)

The sheer scale of the surveillance will become a logistical, ethical, and civil rights nightmare. It will drive everybody clean crazy. And freedom — that precious, precious thing — will be the first casualty. It's already hurt and hemorrhaging dangerously.

Governments across the world are cynically using the prevailing paranoia to promote their own interests. All kinds of unpredictable political forces are being unleashed. In India, for instance, members of the All India People's Resistance Forum who were distributing anti-war and anti-U.S. pamphlets in Delhi have been jailed. Even the printer of the leaflets was arrested. The right-wing government (while it shelters Hindu extremists groups like the Vishva Hindu Parishad and the Bajrang Dal) has banned the Students' Islamic Movement of India and is trying to revive an anti-terrorist act that had been withdrawn after the Human Rights Commission reported that it had been more abused than used. Millions of Indian citizens are Muslim. Can anything be gained by alienating them?

Every day that the war goes on, raging emotions are being let loose into the world. The international press has little or no independent access to the war zone. In any case, the mainstream media, particularly in the United States, has more or less rolled over, allowing itself to be tickled on the stomach with press handouts from military men and government officials. Afghan radio stations have been destroyed by the bombing. The Taliban has always been deeply suspicious of the press. In the propaganda war, there is no accurate estimate of how many people have been killed, or how much destruction has taken place. In the absence of reliable information, wild rumors spread.

Put your ear to the ground in this part of the world, and you can hear the thrumming, the deadly drumbeat of burgeoning anger. Please. Please, stop the war now. Enough people have died. The smart missiles are just not smart enough. They're blowing up whole warehouses of suppressed fury.

President George Bush recently boasted, "When I take action, I'm not going to fire a two million dollar missile at a ten dollar empty tent and hit a camel in the butt. It's going to be decisive." President Bush should know that there are no targets in Afghanistan that will give his missiles their money's worth. Perhaps, if only to balance his books, he should develop some cheaper missiles to use on cheaper targets and cheaper lives in the poor countries of the world. But then, that may not make good business sense to the International Coalition's weapons manufacturers.

It wouldn't make any sense at all, for example, to the Carlyle Group — described by the *Industry Standard* as "one of the world's largest private investment funds," with thirteen billion dollars under management. Carlyle invests in the defense sector and makes its money from military conflicts and weapons spending.

Carlyle is run by men with impeccable credentials. Former U.S. Defense Secretary Frank Carlucci is its Chairman and Managing Director (he was a college roommate of Donald Rumsfeld's). Carlyle's other partners include former U.S. Secretary of State James A. Baker III, George Soros, Fred Malek (George Bush Sr.'s campaign manager).

An American paper — the *Baltimore Chronicle and Sentinel* — says that former President Bush is reported to be seeking investments for the Carlyle Group from Asian markets. He is reportedly paid not inconsiderable sums of money to make "presentations" to potential government clients.

Ho Hum. As the tired saying goes, it's all in the family.

Then there's that other branch of traditional family business — oil. Remember, President George Bush (Jr.) and Vice-President Dick Cheney both made their fortunes working in the U.S. oil industry.

Turkmenistan, which borders the northwest of Afghanistan, holds the world's third-largest gas reserves and an estimated six billion barrels of oil reserves. Enough, experts say, to meet American energy needs for the next thirty years (or a developing country's energy requirements for a couple of centuries.)

America has always viewed oil as a security consideration, and protected it by any means it deems necessary. Few of us doubt that its military presence in the Gulf has little to do with its concern for human rights and almost entirely to do with its strategic interest in oil.

Oil and gas from the Caspian region currently moves northward to European markets. Geographically and politically, Iran and Russia are major impediments to American interests.

In 1998, Dick Cheney — then CEO of Halliburton, a major player in the oil industry — said, "I can't think of a time when we've had a region emerge as suddenly to become as strategically significant as the Caspian. It's almost as if the opportunities have arisen overnight." True enough.

For some years now, an American oil giant called Unocal has been negotiating with the Taliban for permission to construct an oil pipeline through Afghanistan to Pakistan and out to the Arabian Sea. From here, Unocal hopes to access the lucrative "emerging markets" in South and Southeast Asia. In December 1997, a delegation of Taliban mullahs traveled to America and even met U.S. State Department officials and Unocal executives in Houston.

At that time, the Taliban's taste for public executions and its treatment of Afghan women were not made out to be the crimes against humanity that they are now. Over the next six months, pressure from hundreds of outraged American feminist groups was brought to bear on the Clinton administration. Fortunately, they managed to scuttle the deal. And now comes the U.S. oil industry's big chance.

In America, the arms industry, the oil industry, the major media networks, and, indeed, U.S. foreign policy are all controlled by the same business combines. Therefore, it would be foolish to expect this talk of guns and oil and defense deals to get any real play in the media.

In any case, to a distraught, confused people whose pride has just been wounded, whose loved ones have been tragically killed, whose anger is fresh and sharp, the inanities about the "clash of civilizations" and the "good versus evil" home in unerringly. They are cynically doled out by government spokesmen like a daily dose of vitamins or anti-depressants. Regular medication ensures that mainland America continues to remain the enigma it has always been — a curiously insular people, administered by a pathologically meddlesome, promiscuous government.

And what of the rest of us, the numb recipients of this onslaught of what we know to be preposterous propaganda? The daily consumers of the lies and brutality smeared in peanut butter and strawberry jam being air-dropped into our minds just like those yellow food packets. Shall we look away and eat because we're hungry, or shall we stare unblinking at the grim theater unfolding in Afghanistan until we retch collectively and say, in one voice, that we have had enough?

As the first year of the new millennium rushes to a

close, one wonders — have we forfeited our right to dream? Will we ever be able to re-imagine beauty? Will it be possible ever again to watch the slow, amazed blink of a new-born gecko in the sun, or whisper back to the marmot who has just whispered in your ear — without thinking of the World Trade Center and Afghanistan?

GLOSSARY

Adivasi: Tribal, but literally original inhabitants of India.

Babri Masjid: On December 6, 1992, violent mobs of Hindu fundamentalists converged on the town of Ayodhya and demolished the Babri Masjid, an old Muslim mosque. Initiated by the BJP leader L.K. Advani, this was the culmination of a nationwide campaign to "arouse the pride" of Hindus. Plans for replacing it with a huge Hindu temple are under way.

Beedi: A mixture of blended tobacco wrapped in beedi leaves.

Beej Bachao Andolan: A farmers' movement promoting the use of indigenous crops, cropping systems, and agricultural methods.

Bharatiya Janata Party: A Hindu nationalist party (literally, the Indian People's Party).

Dalit: Those who are oppressed or literally "ground down." The preferred term for those people who used to be called "untouchables" in India.

Dharna: Peaceful protest.

EIAs: Environmental Impact Assessments, usually done by private consultants hired by project authorities for projects such as dams, mines, and large-scale irrigation projects.

Goondas: Thugs.

Hydel: Hydroelectric power.

Jain Hawala case: A scandal involving twenty-four politicians charged with taking bribes from businessman Surendra Kumar Jain.

Kahars: A caste whose main occupation is fishing.

Kevats: A caste whose main occupation is plying boats.

Khichdi: A rice and lentil dish.

Koel Karo Sangathan: The Koel Karo Jan Sangathan, a movement against a proposed dam on the Koel and Karo rivers in the State of Bihar.

Kumbh Mela: A Hindu festival in which millions gather to ritually bathe in sacred rivers.

Manusmriti: An ancient code of conduct, attributed to Manu, sometimes viewed as a book of Hindu laws.

Mazdoor Kisan Shakti Sangathan: Literally, Organization for the Empowerment of Workers and Farmers, active in the right-to-information campaigns in Rajasthan.

Naga Sadhu: The naked warrior-ascetics of the Shaiva sect.

Narmada Bachao Andolan: Save the Narmada Movement.

Rashtriya Swayamsevak Sangh (RSS): Literally, the National Self-Help Group. A right-wing militaristic organization with a clearly articulated anti-minority stand and a nationalistic notion of *hindutva.* The RSS is the ideological backbone of the BJP.

Shakha: An RSS branch or center.

Shiv Sena: A rabid right-wing regional Hindu chauvinist party in the State of Maharashtra.

Shloka: Stanzas or verse in general that are prayers to the deities.

Swadeshi: Nationalist.

Tehelka case: An exposé by the Tehelka web site, in which senior Indian politicians, defense officers, and government servants were secretly filmed accepting bribes from journalists posing as arms dealers.

NOTES

(1) Germany is considering changing its immigration laws in order to import Indian software engineers: Roger Cohen, "Germans Seek Foreign Labor For New Era Of Computers," *New York Times,* April 9, 2000, p. 1.

(2) The Naga Sadhu at the Kumbh Mela who towed the District Commissioner's car with his penis: See report at Rediff.com (online at http://www.rediff.com/news/2001/may/26pic3.htm).

(4) Three hundred million people are illiterate: For data on poverty and illiteracy in India, see United Nations Development Program, *Human Development Report 2000: Human Rights and Human Development* (New York: Oxford University Press, 2000), Table 1: Human Development Index, p. 159, Table 4: Human Poverty in Developing Countries, p. 170, and Table 19: Demographic Trends, p. 225. Hereafter UNDP 2000. Reports also available online at http://www.undp.org and at the site of the UNDP Program in India, online at http://www.undp.org.in/.

(10) After writing *The God of Small Things* I wrote three political essays: See Arundhati Roy, *The Cost of Living* (New York: Modern Library, 1999), which includes "The End of the Imagination," published in *Outlook* and *Frontline* magazines in August 1998, and "The End of Imagination," published by *Outlook* and *Frontline* in May–June 1999. "Power Politics: The Reincarnation of Rumpel-

stiltskin," the second chapter in this volume, appeared originally in *Outlook,* November 27, 2000. See http://www.front-lineonline.com and http://www.outlookindia.com/. Arundhati Roy, *The God of Small Things* (New York: HarperPerennial, 1998).

(13) Seven hundred million people live in rural areas: UNDP 2000, Table 19: Demographic Trends, p. 225.

(15) This year government warehouses are overflowing with forty-two million tons of food grain: Ashok Gulati, "Over-flowing Granaries, Empty Stomachs," *The Economic Times of India,* April 27, 2000.

(15) Three hundred and fifty million Indian citizens live below the poverty line: See UNDP 2000, Table 4: Human Poverty in Developing Countries, p. 170, and Table 19: Demographic Trends, p. 225. See also David Gardiner, "Impossible India's Improbable Chance," *The World in 2001* (London: The Economist, 2000), p. 46.

(15) The Indian government lifted import restrictions on 1,400 commodities.... Its agreement with the World Trade Organization: Joseph Kahn, "U.S.-India Agreement," *New York Times,* January 11, 2000, p. 4.

(17) The government is in the process of amending the present Land Acquisition Act: See Dev Raj, "Land Acquisition Bill Worse Than Colonial Law," Inter Press Service, December 3, 1998, and S. Gopikrishna Warrier, "India: NGOs for Including Relief, Rehab Provisions in Land Act," *Business Line,* February 13, 2001.

(19) The Supreme Court permitted the construction of the Sardar Sarovar Dam: Associated Press, "Anti-Dam Activists Vow to Protest India's Supreme Court Ruling," October 20, 2000. For more on the Sardar Sarovar Dam project, see *The Cost of Living,* "The Sardar Sarovar Dam: A Brief Introduction," (on-line at the Friends of the River Narmada web site:

http://www.narmada.org/sardarsarovar.html) and related links; and Sanjay Sangvai, *The River and Life: People's Struggle in the Narmada Valley* (Mumbai and Calcutta: Earthcare Books, 2000).

(19) Four hundred thousand people who would be displaced by the project: See Frederick Noronha, "Dam Protestors Battle Police for Access to World Bank President," Environment News Service, Global News Wire, November 13, 2000.

(20) Big Dams in India have displaced not hundreds, not thousands, but millions: See *The Cost of Living*, p. 17; R. Rangachari et al., "Large Dams: India's Experience: A WCD Case Study Prepared as an Input to the World Commission on Dams," Final Paper: November 2000, World Commission on Dams Country Review Paper, pp. 116-17 and 130-31. Online at http://www.dams.org/studies/in/. Hereafter, Rangachari et al., "Large Dams: India's Experience." For additional information on Big Dams, see Patrick McCully, *Silenced Rivers: The Ecology and Politics of Large Dams,* enlarged and updated edition (London: Zed Books, 2001), and the website of the International Rivers Network at http://www.irn.org/.

(20) Almost half of them are Dalit and Adivasi: For more information on displacement from Sardar Sarovar, see World Commission on Dams, *Dams and Development: A New Framework for Decision-Making: The Report of the World Commission on Dams* (London and Sterling, Virginia: Earthscan, 2000), Box 4.3, p. 104. Hereafter, WCD Report. See also R. Rangachari et al., "Large Dams: India's Experience," pp. 116-17; Planning Commission, Government of India, *Mid-Term Appraisal of the Ninth Five-Year Plan: Final Document (1997-2002)* (Delhi: Planning Commission, 2000), Chapter 4, "Irrigation, Flood Control and Command Area Development: Rehabilitation and Resettlement," p. 89, Paragraph 68 (online at http://planningcommission.nic.in/mta-9702/mta-ch4.pdf); http://www.dams.org/global/india.htm; *The Cost of Living*, p. 18; Bradford Morse and Thomas R. Berger, *Sardar*

Sarovar: The Report of the Independent Review (Ottawa: Resource Futures International, 1992), p. 62; and Government of India, *28th and 29th Report of the Commissioner for Scheduled Castes and Scheduled Tribes* (New Delhi: Government of India, 1988).

(20) Yet India is the only country in the world that refused permission to the World Commission on Dams to hold a public hearing.... threatened members of the commission with arrest: See "Indian Govt to Protest World Commission on Dams Report," *Asia Pulse,* February 5, 2001; Kalpana Sharma, "Misconceptions about Dams Commission," *The Hindu,* September 11, 1998; "Keshubhai Warns Dam Inspection Team May Be Held," *Indian Express,* September 9, 1998; "Gujarat Bans Visit of 'Anti-Dam' Body," *The Hindu,* September 5, 1998; and Kalpana Sharma, "Damning all Dissent," *The Hindu,* September 21, 1998.

(20) The World Commission on Dams report: WCD Report (citation above). See the WCD web site: http://www.dams.org/ and "Medium and Large Dams Damned," *The Business Standard,* September 23, 2000.

(20) Supreme Court ordered the closure of seventy-seven thousand "polluting and nonconforming" industrial units in Delhi: "SC Wants Time Limit on Closure of Polluting Units," *The Times of India,* January 25, 2001. Additional information supplied to the author by Sukumar Muralidharan, *Frontline* magazine's Chief of Bureau in New Delhi, India, based on research from news reports, the Finance Department, and the Delhi Lokatantrik Adhikar Manch.

(21) Close to forty percent of Delhi's population of twelve million ... live in slums and unauthorized colonies: See Peter Popham, "Squalid, Disgusting, Toxic: Is This the Dirtiest City on the Planet?" *The Independent,* October 27, 1997, p. E9, and World Bank, "World Bank Says World's Worst Slums Can Be Transformed," Press Release, June 3, 1996 (online at http://

www.worldbank.org/html/extdr/extme/slumspr.htm).

(22) Sixty-seven percent of Delhi's pollution comes from motor vehicles: Government of India, Ministry of Environment and Forests, *White Paper on Pollution in Delhi: With an Action Plan* (New Delhi: Ministry of Environment and Forests, 1997) (online at http://envfor.nic.in/divisions/cpoll/delpolln.html).

(25) The international dam industry.... is worth thirty-two to forty-six billion U.S. dollars a year: See WCD Report, p. 11., and Table 1.2.

(29) On October 15, 1999, [the Supreme Court] issued an elaborate order: See "NBA Case: Supreme Court Adjourns Hearing on Gujarat Plea," *The Hindu,* July 30, 1999, and T. Padmanabha Rao, "India: Supreme Court Unhappy with NBA Leaders, Arundhati Roy," *The Hindu,* October 16, 1999.

(38) During The Visit, contracts worth about three (some say four) billion U.S. dollars were signed: Stephen Fidler and Khozem Merchant, "US, India Announce Deals of Dollars 4bn," *Financial Times,* March 25, 2000, p. 10.

(38) A Memorandum of Intent signed by the Ogden Energy Group ... and S. Kumars: Peter Popham, "Clinton's Visit Seals Future for Controversial Indian Dam," *The Independent,* March 28, 2000, p. 16, and "S Kumars Ties Up with Ogden for MP Project," *Economic Times of India,* December 14, 1999.

(39) It envisages building three thousand and two hundred dams (thirty big dams, one hundred and thirty-five medium dams, and the rest small).... Lower Paleolithic Age: See *The Cost of Living,* pp. 27-29; WCD Report, p. 117; Steven A. Brandt and Fekri Hassan, "Dams and Cultural Heritage Management: Final Report — August 2000," WCD Working Paper (online at http://www.dams.org/docs/html/contrib/soc212.htm) and WCD, "Flooded Fortunes: Dams and Cultural Heritage Management," Press Release, September 26, 2000 (online at http://www.

dams.org/press/pressrelease_61.htm). See also *New Internationalist* 336 (July 2001): "Do or Die: The People Versus Development in the Narmada Valley" (online at http://www.oneworld.org/ni/issue336/title336.htm) and documentation at the Friends of the River Narmada online at http://www.narmada.org/nvdp.dams/.

(40) On the very days that President Clinton was in India ... the World Water Forum was convened: Second World Water Forum: From Vision to Action, March 17-22, 2000, The Hague. See online report at http://www.worldwaterforum.net/.

(41) One billion people in the world have no access to safe drinking water: UNDP 2000, p. 4.

(43) In a country like India, seventy percent of the population lives in rural areas. That's seven hundred million people: See notes to page 13 above.

(44) Cochabamba: See "Bolivian Water Plan Dropped After Protests Turn Into Melees," *New York Times,* April 11, 2000.

(45) Recently, Jack Welch, the CEO of General Electric (GE), was on TV in India: "Develop Infrastructure to Cope With Digital Revolution: John Welch," *The Hindu,* September 17, 2000, and "Welch Makes a Power Point," *The Economic Times of India,* September 17, 2000. Webcast of Jack Welch's September 16, 2000, speech online at http://www.ge.com/in/webcast.html.

(46) Two hundred million have no access to safe drinking water: See World Resource Institute, *World Resources 1998-1999* (Oxford: Oxford University Press, 1998), p. 251, and UNDP, Table 4: Human Poverty in Developing Countries, p. 170.

(46) Four corporations that dominate the production of power-generation equipment.... at least twenty thousand megawatts of power: Peter Marsh, "Big Four Lead the Field in Power Stakes: The Main Players," *Financial Times,* June 4, 2001, p. 2.

(46) India and China are their big target markets: U.S. Department of Energy, Energy Information Administration, *International Energy Outlook 1998,* Electricity Report (DOE/EIA-0484 [98]). Online at http://www.eia.doe.gov/oiaf/archive/ieo98/ elec.html.

(47) Today BHEL.... is being forced into "joint ventures" ... provide the equipment and the technology: See "India: Bharat Heavy Electricals-GE's Refurbishment Centre," *The Hindu,* March 17, 2001, and "BHEL Net Rises 10% To Rs 599 Crore," *The Economic Times of India,* September 30, 2000.

(47) Almost half the officials named in the major corruption scandal that came to be known as the Jain Hawala case were officials from the power sector: Abhay Mehta, *Power Play: A Study of the Enron Project* (Hyderabad, India: Orient Longman, 2000), p. 15; Irfan Aziz, "The Supreme Court Upheld the Ruling that the Jain Diary Constituted Insufficient Evidence," Rediff.com, July 22, 2000 (online at http://www.rediff.com/news/2000/jul/ 22spec.htm); and Ritu Sarin, "Ex-CBI Official Accuses Vijaya Rama Rao," *Financial Express,* May 11, 1997.

(48) The United States is the single largest foreign investor in the power sector: See figures at "Clinton's India Sojourn: Industry Hopes Doubling of FDI, Better Access to US Markets," March 27, 2000, DHAN.com News Track (online at http:// www.indiaworld.co.in/home/dhan/news/y2k0327-news.html) and George Pickart (Senior Advisor, Bureau for South Asian Affairs), "Address to the Network of South Asian Professionals," Washington, D.C., August 9, 1997 (online at http://www.india-inc.org.in/h0809971.htm).

(48-49): Minister for Power P.R. Kumaramangalam said that the overall figure of loss and deficit in the power sector was 6.7 billion U.S. dollars.... only about a quarter of the electricity that is produced in India is metered: P.R. Kumaramangalam, speech at the Conference of the Power Minister of India, March 2, 2000. See also "India: Power Problems," *Business Line*, June 21, 2000.

(49) According to figures put out by the Power Ministry, the national average T&D losses are twenty-three percent. In 1947, they were 14.39 percent.... like the Dominican Republic, Myanmar, and Bangladesh: Ritu Sarin, "Disappearing Power," *Indian Express,* March 28, 2000 (online at http://www.expressindia.com/ie/daily/20000328/ian28048.html). Hereafter Sarin, "Disappearing Power."

(50) Consider as an example the State of Madhya Pradesh.... seventy percent of the industrialists in the state steal electricity: See Neeraj Mishra, "Megawatt Thieves," *Outlook,* July 31, 2000, p. 54; Sarin, "Disappearing Power"; "India: Power Problems," *Business Line*, June 21, 2000; Louise Lucas, "Survey — India: Delays And Bureaucracy Force Investors To Flee: Power," *Financial Times*, November 6, 2000; and "India's Power Generation To Increase Over Next 3 Years: Minister," *Asia Pulse*, April 27, 2001.

(50) States like Orissa, Andhra Pradesh, and Delhi have T&D losses of between thirty and fifty percent: Sarin, "Disappearing Power"; "Red Tape and Blue Sparks," *The Economist* 359/8224 (June 2-8, 2001), "A Survey of India's Economy," pp. 9-10; and Sunil Saraf, "At Last, The Selloff Gets Underway," *Financial Times,* Survey — Power in Asia 1996, September 16, 1996, p. 5.

(53) The fish bowl of the drive to privatize power, its truly star turn, is the story of Enron, the Houston-based natural gas company: See Abhay Mehta, *Power Play;* Human Rights Watch, *The Enron Corporation: Corporate Complicity in Human Rights Violations* (New York: Human Rights Watch, 1999) (online at http://www.hrw.org/reports/1999/enron/enron-toc.htm); Tony Allison, "Enron's Eight-Year Power Struggle in India," Asia Times Online, January 18, 2001 (online at http://www. atimes.com/reports/CA13Ai01.html); Scott Baldauf, "Plug Pulled on

Investment in India," *Christian Science Monitor,* July 9, 2001, p. 9; S.N. Vasuki, "The Search for a Middle Ground," *Business Times* (Singapore), August 6, 1993; Agence France-Presse, "Work to Start in December on India's Largest Power Plant," September 14, 1993; and Agence France-Presse, "Work on Enron Power Project to Resume on May 1," February 23, 1996.

(53) Home Minister L.K. Advani attacked the phenomenon he called "loot-through-liberalization": Scott Neuman, "More Power Reviews Likely In India," United Press International, August 5, 1995.

(54) Enron had made no secret of the fact that, in order to secure the deal, it had paid out millions of dollars to "educate" the politicians: Agence France-Presse, "India, Enron Deny Payoff Charges Over Axed Project," August 7, 1995, which acknowledges "a remark by an Enron official that the company spent 20 million dollars on 'educating Indians' about the controversial deal."

(54) U.S. Ambassador Frank Wisner.... joined Enron as a director: See "Former US Amabassdor to India Joins Enron Oil Board," *Asia Pulse,* October 30, 1997; Girish Kuber, "US Delegation to Meet Ministers on Enron Row," *The Economic Times of India,* January 23, 2001; and Vijay Prashad, "The Power Elite: Enron and Frank Wisner," *People's Democracy*, November 16, 1997 (online at http://www.igc.org/trac/feature/india/profiles/enron/enronwisner.html).

(54) In November 1995, the BJP–Shiv Sena Government of Maharashtra announced a "re-negotiation" committee.... on terms that would astound the most hard-boiled cynic: See Mark Nicholson, "Elections Cloud Investment in India: Opening the Economy Has Wide Support Despite Recent Events," *Financial Times*, August 21, 1995; Agence France-Presse, "Hindu Leader Ready for Talks on Scrapped Enron Project," August 31, 1995;

BBC Summary of World Broadcasts, "Maharashtra Government Might Consider New Enron Proposal," September 2, 1995; Suzanne Goldenberg, "India Calls On Left Bloc As BJP Cedes Power," *The Guardian*, May 29, 1996; Mark Niicholson, "Delhi Clears Way for Dollars 2.5bn Dabhol Power Plant," *Financial Times*, July 10, 1996, p. 4; and Associated Press, "Enron Can Resume Big Indian Power Project," *New York Times*, July 10, 1996, p. D19.

(54-55) The impugned contract had involved annual payments to Enron of four hundred and thirty million U.S. dollars for Phase I.... The official return on equity is more than thirty percent: See Mehta, *Power Play*, pp. xv, 20-21, and 151-58; Agence France-Presse, "Massive US-Backed Power Project Awaits Indian Court Ruling," August 25, 1996; Kenneth J. Cooper, "Foreign Power Plant Blooms; Low-Key India Venture Avoids Enron's Woes," *International Herald Tribune*, September 11, 1996; Praful Bidwai, "Enron Judgment: Blow to Energy Independence," *The Times of India*, May 22, 1997; and Praful Bidwai, "The Enron Deal Must Go: Albatross Round Public's Neck," *The Times of India*, May 4, 1995.

(55-56) In May 1997, the Supreme Court of India refused to entertain an appeal against Enron: Agence France-Presse, "Enron Power Project Survives Court Challenge," May 3, 1997.

(56) The power that the Enron plant produces is twice as expensive as its nearest competitor and seven times as expensive as the cheapest electricity available in Maharashtra: See "The Dabhol Backlash," *Business Line*, December 5, 2000; Sucheta Dalal, "No Power May End Up Being Better Than That High Cost Power," *Indian Express*, December 3, 2000 (online at http://www.indian-express.com/ie/daily/20001207/sucheta.htm); Soma Banerjee, "State Plans to Move Court on Tariff Revision Proposal," *Economic Times of India*, May 26, 2000; Madhu Nainan, "Indian State Says It Has No Money to Pay Enron for Power," Agence

France-Presse, January 8, 2001; Khozem Merchant, "Enron Invokes Guarantee to Retrieve Fees from Local Unit," *Financial Times,* January 31, 2001, p. 7; S.N. Roy, "The Shocking Truth About Power Reforms," *Indian Express,* February 28, 2000; and Anthony Spaeth, "Bright Lights, Big Bill," *Time* (Asian edition) 157: 8 (February 26, 2001) (online at http://www.time.com/time/asia/biz/magazine/0,9754,99899,00.html).

(56) In May 2000, the Maharashtra Electricity Regulatory Committee (MERC) ruled that temporarily ... no power should be bought from Enron: "India: Maharashtra State Electricity Board Stops Buying Power," *The Hindu,* May 30, 2001; Celia W. Dugger, "High-Stakes Showdown: Enron's Fight Over Power Plant Reverberates Beyond India," *New York Times,* March 20, 2001, p. C1. Hereafter Dugger, "High-Stakes Showdown."

(57) According to the MSEB's calculations, from January 2002 onward, even if it were to buy ninety percent of Enron's output, its losses will amount to 1.2 billion U.S. dollars a year.... more than sixty percent of India's annual Rural Development budget: See Mehta, *Power Play,* p. 3; Dugger, "High-Stakes Showdown"; "Red Tape and Blue Sparks," *The Economist* 359/8224 (June 2-8, 2001), "A Survey of India's Economy," pp. 9-10; Government of India, *Ninth Five Year Plan, 1997-2002* (online at http://www.nic.in/ninthplan/); and Government of India, Press Information Bureau, Fact Sheet (online at http://pib.nic.in/archive/factsheet/fs2000/planning.html).

(57-58) In January 2001, the Maharashtra government (the Congress Party is back in power with a new Chief Minister) announced that it did not have the money to pay Enron's bills.... it would have to auction the government properties named as collateral security in the contract: See S. Balakrishnan, "FIS in U.S. Press Panic Button as MSEB Fails to Pay Enron," *The Times of India,* January 7, 2001; Madhu Nainan, "Indian State Says It Has No Money to Pay Enron for Power," Agence France-Presse,

January 8, 2001; and Khozem Merchant, "Enron Invokes Guarantee to Retrieve Fees from Local Unit," *Financial Times,* January 31, 2001, p. 7.

(58) Enron has friends in high places: See Pratap Chatterjee, "Meet Enron, Bush's Biggest Contributor," *The Progressive* 64: 9 (September 2000) (online at http://www.theprogressive.org/pc0900.htm). See also Dugger, "High-Stakes Showdown."

(58) Former U.S. Ambassador (Richard Celeste this time) publicly chastised the Maharashtra Chief Minister for reneging on payments: Dugger, "High-Stakes Showdown," and Praful Bidwai, "Congentrix = (Equals) Bullying Tricks," *Kashmir Times,* December 27, 1999.

(59) Seventy percent of rural households still have no electricity.... mostly Dalit and Adivasi households, have no electricity: Center for Science and Environment, *State of India's Environment: The Citizens' Fifth Report: Part II: Statistical Database* (New Delhi: Center for Science and Environment, 1999), p. 203; Union Power Minister Suresh Prabhu, Press Conference, Hyderabad, cited in *Business Line,* July 21, 2001; and Abusaleh Shariff, *India: Human Development Report: A Profile of Indian States in the 1990s* (New Delhi: National Council of Applied Economic Research/Oxford University Press, 1999), p. 238.

(60) Today, India pays back more money in interest and repayment installments than it receives. It is forced to incur new debts in order to repay old ones: UNDP 2000, Table 18: Aid and Debt by Recipient Country, p. 221. See also ENS Economic Bureau, "India Inching Towards Debt Trap," *Indian Express,* February 23, 1999 (online at http://www.expressindia.com/ie/daily/19990223/ibu23045.html). See also Economist Intelligence Unit, "India: External Debt" (online at http://www.eiu.com/latest/564449.asp).

(62) The international dam industry alone is worth thirty-two to

forty-six billion U.S. dollars a year: see notes to page 25 above.

(63) India has the third largest number of Big Dams in the world…. forty percent of all the Big Dams being built in the world are being built in India: See *The Cost of Living*, pp. 13-14; WCD Report, Table 1.1: Dams Currently Under Construction, p. 10, and Table V.1: Top 20 Countries by Number of Large Dams, p. 370; and the web site of the International Commission on Large Dams at http://genepi.louis-jean.com/cigb/anglais.html.

(63) Jawaharlal Nehru's famous speech about Big Dams being "the temples of modern India": C.V.J. Sharma, ed., *Modern Temples of India: Selected Speeches of Jawaharlal Nehru at Irrigation and Power Projects* (Delhi: Central Board of Irrigation and Power, 1989), pp. 40-49. See *The Cost of Living*, pp. 7, 13.

(63-64) Mr. Advani said that the three greatest achievements…. "those who do not wish to see India becoming strong in security and socio-economic development": PTI News Agency (New Delhi), "India: Construction Begins on 'Controversial' Narmada Dam," BBC Worldwide Monitoring, October 31, 2000; Vinay Kumar, "People Cheer As Work on Narmada Dam Resumes," *The Hindu*, November 1, 2000; "Violence Mars Gujarat Govt's Narmada Bash," *The Times of India*, November 1, 2000; and "Ministers Attacked, Cars Burnt at Narmada Dam Site," *Hindustan Times*, November 1, 2000.

(65) Ninety percent of the Big Dams in India are irrigation dams: WCD Fact Sheet, "Dams and Water: Global Statistics: India: 4,291 Large Dams and 9% of the World Dam Population" (on-line at http://www.dams.org/global/india.htm). See also Himanshu Thakker, "Performance of Large Dams in India: The Case of Irrigation and Flood Control," paper presented at the World Commission on Dams Regional Consultation, Sri Lanka,

December 1998 (online at http://www.dams.org/submissions/sub_sa91.htm).

(65) India Country Study section in the World Commission on Dams Report: R. Rangachari et al., "Large Dams: India's Experience."

(65-66) One of the chapters in the study deduces that the contribution of large dams to India's food grain produce is less than ten percent: R. Rangachari et al., "Large Dams: India's Experience," p. 25.

(66) This year, more than double that amount is rotting in government storehouses while at the same time three hundred and fifty million Indian citizens live below the poverty line: See Ashok Gulati, "Overflowing Granaries, Empty Stomachs," *The Economic Times of India,* April 27, 2000, and UNDP 2000, Table 4: Human Poverty in Developing Countries, p. 170.

(66) The Ministry of Food and Civil Supplies says that ten percent of India's total food grain produce every year is spoiled or eaten by rats: Gail Omvedt, "The Hindu-Editorial: Rotting Food," *The Hindu*, October 23, 1999. See also Shri Sriram Chuahan, Minister of States for Food and Public Distribution, Ministry of Consumer Affairs, Food, and Public Distribution, "Loss of Foodgrains," Press Release, Government of India, August 8, 2000.

(68) My very conservative estimate of the number of people displaced by Big Dams in India over the last fifty years was thirty-three million people.... the figure could be as high as fifty-six million people: See *The Cost of Living,* p. 17, and notes to page 20 above; and R. Rangachari et al., "Large Dams: India's Experience," p. 116.

(68) Almost half of them are Dalit and Adivasi: see notes to page 20 above.

(69) More than three million acres of submerged forest.... two hundred million Indians have no access to safe drinking water: See notes to page 46 above; *The Cost of Living*, pp. ix, 14, 68-69; and R. Rangachari et al., "Large Dams: India's Experience," p. 132.

(70) The Bargi Dam.... cost ten times more than was budgeted and submerged three times more land than engineers said it would: See "The Human Cost of the Bargi Dam" (online at http://www.narmada.org/nvdp.dams/bargi/bargi.html); and "Dam Ousters to Go on Hunger-Strike," *The Statesman*, August 13, 1997.

(71) Narmada Control Authority had estimated.... "resettlement colonies" ... were also submerged: See WCD Report, pp. 106-107; Sangvai, *The River and Life*, p. 28; and "The Human Cost of the Bargi Dam."

(71) Narmada Sagar Dam, which will submerge two hundred and fifty-one villages: See *The Cost of Living*, p. 35.

(72) Sardar Sarovar Dam will displace close to half a million people.... [and] submerge thirty-two thousand acres of deciduous forest: See WCD Report, pp. 104-105; *The Cost of Living*, pp. 33-35; Robert Marquand, "Indian Dam Protests Evoke Gandhi," *Christian Science Monitor*, August 5, 1999, p. 1; "The Sardar Sarovar Dam: A Brief Introduction" (online at the Friends of the River Narmada web site: http://www.narmada.org/sardarsarovar. html); and Narmada Bachao Andolan (NBA), "Displacement, Submergence and Rehabilitation in Sardar Sarovar Project: Ground Reality Indicating Utter Injustice (online at http://www.narmada. org/sardar-sarovar/sc.ruling/Displacement.rehab. html); and Free the Narmada Campaign, India, "Who Pays? Who Profits? A Short Guide to the Sardar Sarovar Project" (online at http://www. narmada.org/sardar-sarovar/faq/whopays.html).

(72-73): In 1985, before a single study had been done…. the people of the valley forced the bank to withdraw from the project: See International Rivers Network, "Confidential World Bank Evaluation Admits Future of Narmada Dam Uncertain," Press Release, May 16, 1995 (online at http://www.irn.org/programs/narmada/irnwboedmemo950516.html); Office of Director-General, Operations Evaluation, World Bank, "Memorandum to the Executive Directors and the President," March 29, 1995 (online at http://www.irn.org/programs/narmada/ wboedmemo950329.html); and MNC Masala, "The World Bank and Sardar Sarovar Project: A Story of Unacceptable Means Towards Unacceptable Ends," CorpWatch (online at http://www.corpwatch.org/trac/feature/india/profiles/wb/wb13.html); WCD Report, p. 26; and Bradford Morse and Thomas R. Berger, *Sardar Sarovar: The Report of the Independent Review* (Ottawa: Resource Futures International, 1992).

(73) The Supreme Court lifted the injunction: See Celia W. Dugger, "Opponents of India Dam Project Bemoan Green Light From Court," *New York Times*, October 20, 2000, p. A9.

(74) The Madhya Pradesh government has stated on oath that it has no land to resettle "oustees": Free the Narmada Campaign, India, "Who Pays? Who Profits?"

(75): In 1994, the project cost of the Maheshwar Dam was estimated at ninety-nine million U.S. dollars…. Today it stands at four hundred and sixty-seven million: See "The Maheshwar Dam: A Brief Introduction" and related links (online at http://www.narmada.org/maheshwar.html); Meena Menon, "Damned by the People: The Maheshwar Hydro-Electricity Project in Madhya Pradesh," *Business Line*, June 15, 1998; Sangvai, *The River and Life,* pp. 81-84; and Richard E. Bissell, Shekhar Singh, and Hermann Warth, *Maheshwar Hydroelectric Project: Resettlement and Rehabilitation: An Independent Review Conducted for the Ministry of Economic Cooperation and Development (BMZ), Gov-*

ernment of Germany, June 15, 2000 (online at http://www.bmz. de/medien/misc/maheshwar_report.pdf). Hereafter Bissell Report.

(75-76) According to the NBA's calculations…. most of the supply will be generated when it's least needed: See "Mardana Resolution" (online at http://www.narmada.org/maheshwar/ mardana.declaration.html); NBA Press Note, "Hundreds of Maheshwar Dam Affected People Demonstrate at IFCI, Delhi," November 16, 2000 (online at http://www.narmada.org/ nba-press-releases/november-2000/ifci.demo.html); and Sangvai, *The River and Life,* Annexure 4, pp. 194-97, and Annexure 6, pp. 200-201.

(76) According to government surveys, the reservoir of the Maheshwar Dam will submerge sixty-one villages. Thirteen will be wholly submerged: See Heffa Schücking, "The Maheshwar Dam in India," March 1999 (online at http://www. narmada.org/urg990421.3.html).

(79): Jalud is the first of the sixty-one villages slated for submergence in the reservoir of the dam: See Meena Menon, "Damned by the People: The Maheshwar Hydro-Electricity Project in Madhya Pradesh," *Business Line,* June 15, 1998.

(80) After their James Bond campaign with Pierce Brosnan, they've signed India's biggest film star — Hrithik Roshan: See "S. Kumars Forays into Ready-to-Wear Apparel," *India Info,* December 10, 2000, and "S Kumars Ups Ads-Spend by 66% with Kapil Dev on Board," *India Express,* July 8, 1999.

(80) Over the last two years, tens of thousands of villagers have captured the dam site several times and halted construction work: See Meena Menon, "Damned by the People: The Maheshwar Hydro-Electricity Project in Madhya Pradesh," *Business Line,* June 15, 1998, and *New Internationalist* 336.

(80) Protests in the region forced two companies, Bayernwerk and VEW of Germany, to withdraw from the project: See "German Firms Pull Out of MP Dam Project," *The Statesman*, April 21, 1999. See also Desikan Thirunarayanapuram, "Siemens Role in Dam Project Doubtful," *The Statesman*, June 30, 2000.

(80) The German Ministry of Economic Co-operation and Development sent in a team of experts: See Bissell Report.

(81) At the end of August, Siemens withdrew its application for a Hermes guarantee: See "Leaked Letter Shows German Company Quits Bid for Dam Credit," *Deutsche Presse-Agentur*, August 25, 2000, and "US Firm Pulls Out Of Narmada Hydel Project," *The Statesman*, December 13, 2000.

(81) S. Kumars was part of the Indian Prime Minister's business entourage when he visited the United States: "PM's Is Going to Be a 'Power Trip,'" *Indian Express*, September 4, 2000.

(81) Now Ogden has withdrawn: "Ogden Pulls Out from Maheshwar Hydel Unit," *Indian Express*, Friday, December 8, 2000.

(83) In a Call Center College ... groomed to staff the backroom operations of giant transnational companies: See Mark Landler, "Hi, I'm in Bangalore (But I Can't Say So)," *New York Times*, March 21, 2001, p. A1.

(84) From all accounts, call centers are billed to become a multibillion-dollar industry: See David Gardiner, "Impossible India's Improbable Chance," *The World in 2001* (London: The Economist, 2000), p. 46.

(84) Recently the giant Tata industrial group ... "picking up [the] American accent and slang": See Prabhakar Sinha, "Tatas Plan Foray Into Call Centre Business," *The Times of India*, October 7, 2000.

(101) The Tehelka tapes broadcast: See Nadja Vancauwen-

berghe and Maurice Frank, "New Media: If You Take a Bribe, We'll Nail You," *The Guardian,* June 4, 2001; "Egg On Congress's Face," *The Statesman,* April 10, 2001; "Chief Justice Turns Down Request for Sitting Judge for Arms Scandal Inquiry," BBC Summary of World Broadcasts, March 20, 2001; and "CJI Refuses to Spare Sitting Judge," *The Times of India,* March 20, 2001.

(102) Chief Justice of India refused to allow a sitting judge to head the judicial enquiry into the Tehelka scandal: See PTI, "Ex-SC Judge to Hold Probe," *The Tribune,* March 19, 2001 (online at http://www.tribuneindia.com/20010320/main3.htm).

(105) In the aftermath ... Then he broke down and wept: Fox News, September 17, 2001.

(106) The FBI said that it had doubts ... which governments were supporting them: Marc Levine, "New Suspect Arrested, But Doubts Grow Over Terrorists' Identities," Agence France-Presse, September 21, 2001.

(107) In his September 20 address ... disagree with each other: President George W. Bush, Address to Joint Session of Congress, September 11, 2001, "The Terrorist Attacks on the United States," Federal News Service, September 20, 2001.

(110) Fifteen million square feet of office space: See Elsa Brenner, "Hoping to Fill the Need for Office Space," *New York Times (Westchester Weekly Edition),* September 23, 2001, p. 3.

(111) It was "a very hard choice," but ... "we think the price is worth it": Leslie Stahl, "Punishing Saddam," produced by Catherine Olian, CBS, *60 Minutes,* May 12, 1996.

(112) Among them, half a million maimed orphans: See Tamim Ansary, "Bomb Afghanistan Back to Stone Age? It's Been Done," *Providence Journal-Bulletin,* September 22, 2001, p. B7.

(112) The countryside is littered with land mines ... most recent estimate: Thomas E. Ricks, "Land Mines, Aging Missiles Pose

Threat," *Washington Post,* September 25, 2001, p. A15. See also Danna Harman, "Digging up Angola's Deadly Litter," *Christian Science Monitor,* July 27, 2001, p. 6.

(112) UN estimates ... emergency aid: See Barry Bearak, "Misery Hangs Over Afghanistan After Years of War and Drought," *New York Times,* September 24, 2001, p. B3; Rajiv Chandrasekaran and Pamela Constable, "Panicked Afghans Flee to Border Area," *Washington Post,* September 23, 2001, p. A30; Catherine Solyom, "Exhibit a Glimpse Into Refugee Life," *The Gazette* (Montreal), September 21, 2001, p. A13; and Raymond Whitaker, Agence France-Presse, "Pakistan Fears for Seven Million Refugees as Winter Looms," *The Independent* (London), September 27, 2001, p. 4.

(113) One of the worst humanitarian disasters of recent times: BBC, "Aid Shortage Adds to Afghan Woes," September 22, 2001. Available online at http://news.bbc.co.uk/hi/english/world/south_asia/newsid_1556000/1556117.stm.

(113) "Bombing Afghanistan back to the stone age": See Tamim Ansary, "Bomb Afghanistan Back to Stone Age? It's Been Done," *Providence Journal-Bulletin,* September 22, 2001, p. B7.

(113) A run on maps: See Paul Leavitt, "Maps of Afghanistan Now in Short Supply," *USA Today,* September 18, 2001, p. 13A.

(113) CIA's largest covert operation since the Vietnam War: *Washington Post,* February 7, 1985, quoted in Raja Anwar, *The Tragedy of Afghanistan: A First-Hand Account,* trans. Khalid Hasan (New York and London: Verso, 1988), p. 232; "Inside the Taliban: U.S. Helped Cultivate the Repressive Regime Sheltering bin Laden," *Seattle Times,* September 19, 2001, p. A3; and Andrew Duffy, "Geographic Warriors," *Ottawa Citizen,* September 23, 2001, p. C4.

(114) CIA funded and recruited ... proxy war: On the CIA connection, see Steve Coll, "Anatomy of a Victory: CIA's Covert

Afghan War," *Washington Post,* July 19, 1992, p. A1; Steve Coll, "In CIA's Covert Afghan War, Where to Draw the Line Was Key," *Washington Post,* July 20, 1992, p. A1; Tim Weiner, "Blowback From the Afghan Battlefield," *New York Times Magazine,* March 13, 1994, p. 6: 53; and Ahmed Rashid, "The Making of a Terrorist," *Straits Times* (Singapore), September 23, 2001, p. 26.

(114) Forced farmers to plant opium: See Scott Baldauf, "Afghans Try Opium-Free Economy," *Christian Science Monitor,* April 3, 2001, p. 1.

(114) Profits ... ploughed back into training and arming militants: See David Kline, "Asia's 'Golden Crescent' Heroin Floods the West," *Christian Science Monitor,* November 9, 1982, p. 1; David Kline, "Heroin's Trail from Poppy Fields to the West," *Christian Science Monitor,* November 10, 1982, p. 1; and Rahul Bedi, "The Assassins and Drug Dealers Now Helping US Intelligence," *Daily Telegraph* (London), September 26, 2001, p. 10.

(115) Funded by the ISI ... cohort of the CIA: See Peter Popham, "Taliban Monster That Was Launched by the US," *The Independent* (London), September 17, 2001, p. 4.

(115) Sharia laws ... buried alive: See Suzanne Goldenberg, "Mullah Keeps Taliban on a Narrow Path," *Guardian* (London), August 17, 1998, p. 12.

(116) Number of heroin addicts grew ... massive number: See David K. Willis, "Pakistan Seeks Help from Abroad to Stem Heroin Flow," *Christian Science Monitor,* February 28, 1984, p. 11.

(116) Pakistan's economy is crumbling: See Farhan Bokhari, "Pakistan: Living in Shadow of Debt Mountain," *Financial Times* (London), March 6, 2001, Survey: Pakistan, p. 4.

(116-117) Taliban ... Pakistan's own political parties: See Douglas Frantz, "Sentiment in Pakistani Town Is Ardently

Pro-Taliban," *New York Times,* September 27, 2001, p. B1, and Rahul Bedi, "The Assassins and Drug Dealers Now Helping US Intelligence," *Daily Telegraph* (London), September 26, 2001, p. 10.

(117) Musharraf ... civil war on his hands: See Edward Luce, "Pakistan Nervousness Grows as Action Nears," *Financial Times* (London), September 27, 2001, p. 6.

(117) Indian goverment ... rather than Pakistan: See Angus Donald and Khozem Merchant, "Concern at India's Support for US," *Financial Times* (London), September 21, 2001, p. 14.

(118) Warnings ... crop duster: See Jeff Greenfield and David Ensor, "America's New War: Weapons of Terror," CNN, *Greenfield at Large,* September 24, 2001.

(119) "Rid the world of evildoers": See Jim Drinkard, "Bush Vows to 'Rid the World of Evildoers,'" *USA Today,* September 17, 2001, p. 1A.

(119-120) Donald Rumsfeld ... he would consider it a victory: Secretary of Defense Donald Rumsfeld, Special Defense Briefing, "Developments Concerning Attacks on the Pentagon and the World Trade Center Last Week," Federal News Service, September 20, 2001.

(120) Seventeen thousand killed ... in 1982: See Robert Fisk, "This Is Not a War on Terror, It's a Fight Against America's Enemies," *The Independent* (London), September 25, 2001, p. 4.

(121) Someone recently said ... had to invent him: George Monbiot, "The Need for Dissent," *Guardian* (London), September 18, 2001, p. 17.

(121) Produce evidence ... court of law: See Michael Slackman, "Terrorism Case Illustrates Difficulty of Drawing Tangible Ties to Al Qaeda," *Los Angeles Times,* September 22, 2001, p. A1.

(121) "CEO of the holding company": See Tim Russert, "Secre-

tary of State Colin Powell Discusses America's Preparedness for the War on Terrorism," NBC, *Meet the Press,* September 23, 2001.

(122) Bush's response ... "non-negotiable": See T. Christian Miller, "A Growing Global Chorus Calls for Proof," *Los Angeles Times,* September 24, 2001, p. A10, and Dan Rather, "President Bush's Address to Congress and the Nation," CBS, *CBS News Special Report,* September 20, 2001.

(122) Bhophal gas leak ... sixteen thousand people: See Nityanand Jayaraman and Peter Popham, "Work Halts at Indian Unilever Factory After Poisoning Alert," *The Independent* (London), March 11, 2001, p. 19.

(122) "Full spectrum dominance": See Jack Hitt, "Battlefield: Space," *New York Times Magazine,* August 5, 2001, p. 6: 30.

(123) Bush administration ... "war on drugs": See Colin Nickerson and Indira A.R. Lakshmanan, "America Prepares the Global Dimension," *Boston Globe,* September 27, 2001, p. A1; Barbara Crossette, "Taliban's Ban On Poppy A Success, U.S. Aides Say," *New York Times,* May 20, 2001, p. 1: 7; and Christopher Hitchens, "Against Rationalization," *The Nation* 273: 10 (October 8, 2001), p. 8.

(124) "Either you are with us or you are with the terrorists": President George W. Bush, Address to Joint Session of Congress, "September 11, 2001, Terrorist Attacks on the United States," Federal News Service, September 20, 2001.

(125) Stealth bombers ... high drag bombs: See Alexander Nicoll, "US Warplanes Can Attack at All Times, Says Forces Chief," *Financial Times* (London), October 10, 2001, p. 2.

(125) "We will behave multilaterally ... when we must": See Noam Chomsky, "US Iraq Policy: Motives and Consequences," in *Iraq Under Siege: The Deadly Impact of Sanctions and War* (Cambridge: South End Press; London: Pluto Press, 2000), p. 54.

(126) Stand up in a court of law: See Michael Slackman, "Terrorism Case Illustrates Difficulty of Drawing Tangible Ties to Al Qaeda," *Los Angeles Times,* September 22, 2001, p. A1.

(127) "We are a peaceful nation" ... "We are a peaceful people": "Bush's Remarks on U.S. Military Strikes on Afghanistan," *New York Times,* October 8, 2001, p. B6, and Ellen Hale, "'To Safeguard Peace, We Have to Fight,' Blair Emphasizes to Britons," *USA Today,* October 8, 2001, p. 6A.

(128) "This is the calling ... And we will not tire": George W. Bush, "Remarks by President George W. Bush at an Anti-Terrorism Event," Washington, D.C., Federal News Service, October 10, 2001.

(130) Between the Soviet Union ... poured into Afghanistan: See Tom Pelton, "A Graveyard for Many Armies," *Baltimore Sun,* September 18, 2001, p. 2A.

(131) One and a half million ... this new war: See Dave Newbart, "Nowhere to Go But Up," *Chicago Sun-Times,* September 18, 2001, p. 10.

(131) By the second day ... assigned payload of bombs: See Edward Epstein, "U.S. Seizes Skies Over Afghanistan," *San Francisco Chronicle,* October 10, 2001, p. A1.

(131) One senior official ... "not a target-rich environment": See Steven Mufson, "For Bush's Veteran Team, What Lessons to Apply?" *Washington Post,* September 15, 2001, p. A5.

(131-132) Rumsfeld ... laughter in the briefing room: Donald H. Rumsfeld, "Defense Department Special Briefing Re: Update on U.S. Military Campaign in Afghanistan," Arlington, Virginia, Federal News Service, October 9, 2001.

(132) By the third day ... "achieved air supremacy over Afghanistan": Edward Epstein, "U.S. Seizes Skies Over Afghanistan," *San Francisco Chronicle,* October 10, 2001, p. A1.

(132) For the archives ... is being glossed over: Human Rights Watch, "Military Assistance to the Afghan Opposition," Human Rights Watch Backgrounder, October 2001. Available on-line at http://www.hrw.org/backgrounder/asia/afghan-bck1005.htm. See also Gregg Zoroya, "Northern Alliance has Bloody Past, Critics Warn," *USA Today,* October 12, 2001, p. 1A.

(132) Ahmed Shah ... September 2001: See David Rohde, "Visit to Town Where 2 Linked to bin Laden Killed Afghan Rebel," *New York Times,* September 26, 2001, p. B4.

(132-133) Northern Alliance ... topple the Taliban: See Zahid Hussain and Stephen Farrell, "Tribal Chiefs See Chance to Be Rid of Taleban," *The Times* (London), October 2, 2001.

(133) "Restoring" the kingdom ... since 1973: See Alan Cowell, "Afghan King Is Courted and Says, 'I Am Ready,'" *New York Times,* September 26, 2001, p. A4.

(133) Reports have begun ... civilian casualties: See Said Mohammad Azam, "Civilian Toll Mounts as Bush Signals Switch to Ground Assault," Agence France-Presse, October 19, 2001; Indira A. R. Lakshmanan, "UN's Peaceful Mission Loses 4 to War," *Boston Globe,* October 10, 2001, p. A1; and Steven Lee Myers and Thom Shanker, "Pilots Told to Fire at Will in Some Zones," *New York Times,* October 17, 2001, p. B2.

(133-134) Those who have experience ... course of this winter: See U.N. documents and reports summarized in Center for Economic and Social Rights, "Afghanistan Fact Sheet 3: Key Human Vulnerabilities." Available on-line at http://www.cesr.org.

(134) Airdropping food packets ... land mines: See David Rising, "U.S. Military Defends Its Food Drops in Afghanistan from Criticism by Aid Organizations," Associated Press, October 10, 2001; Luke Harding, "Taliban Say Locals Burn Food Parcels," *Guardian* (London), October 11, 2001, p. 9; Tyler Marshall and

Megan Garvey "Relief Efforts Trumped by Air War," *Los Angeles Times,* October 17, 2001, p. A1.

(134-135) Their contents ... user instructions: Martin Merzer and Jonathan S. Landay, Knight Ridder News Service, "Second Phase of Strikes Begins," *Milwaukee Journal Sentinel,* October 10, 2001, p. 1A.

(135-136) Rudi Giuliani ... the Middle East: Jennifer Steinhauer, "Citing Comments on Attack, Giuliani Rejects Saudi's Gift," *New York Times,* October 12, 2001, p. B13.

(137) Reagan praised them as freedom fighters: See Robert Pear, "Arming Afghan Guerrillas: A Huge Effort Led by U.S.," *New York Times,* April 18, 1988, p. A1. See also Steve Coll, "Anatomy of a Victory: CIA's Covert Afghan War," *Washington Post,* July 19, 1992, p. A1; Steve Coll, "In CIA's Covert Afghan War, Where to Draw the Line Was Key," *Washington Post,* July 20, 1992, p. A1; Tim Weiner, "Blowback From the Afghan Battlefield," *New York Times Magazine,* March 13, 1994, p. 6: 53; and Ahmed Rashid, "The Making of a Terrorist," *Straits Times* (Singapore), September 23, 2001, p. 26.

(139) In India ... printer of the leaflets was arrested: See "Voices of Dissent and Police Action," *The Hindu,* October 13, 2001.

(139) Right-wing government ... anti-terrorist act: See "Vajpayee Gets Tough, Says No Compromise with Terrorism," *Economic Times of India,* October 15, 2001.

(140) "When I take action ... be decisive": See Howard Fineman, "A President Finds His True Voice," *Newsweek,* September 24, 2001. p. 50.

(141) Carlyle Group ... thirteen billion dollars under management: See Aaron Pressman, "Former FCC Head Follows the Money," The Industry Standard.com, May 2, 2001.

(141) Carlyle is run by men ... government clients: See Alice

Power Politics

Cherbonnier, "Republican-Controlled Carlyle Group Poses Serious Ethical Questions for Bush Presidents, but *Baltimore Sun* Ignores It," *Baltimore Chronicle and Sentinel* On-line. Available at http://www.charm.net/~marc/chronicle/media3_oct01.shtml. See also Leslie Wayne, "Elder Bush in Big G.O.P. Cast Toiling for Top Equity Firm," *New York Times,* March 5, 2001, p. A1.

(142) Turkmenistan ... couple of centuries: See Editorial, "America, Oil and Afghanistan," *The Hindu,* October 13, 2001.

(142-143) "I can't think of a time ... arisen overnight": See Tyler Marshall, "The New Oil Rush: High Stakes in the Caspian," *Los Angeles Times,* February 23, 1998, p. A1.

(143) An American oil giant ... executives in Houston: See Ahmed Rashid, *Taliban: Militant Islam, Oil and Fundamentalism in Central Asia* (New Haven: Yale Nota Bene/Yale University Press, 2001), pp. 143-82.

INDEX

ABOUT THE AUTHOR

Arundhati Roy was trained as an architect. She is the author of the novel *The God of Small Things*, for which she received the Booker Prize, and *The Cost of Living*. Roy lives in New Delhi, India.

ABOUT SOUTH END PRESS

South End Press is a nonprofit, collectively run book publisher with more than 200 titles in print. Since our founding in 1977, we have tried to meet the needs of readers who are exploring, or are already committed to, the politics of radical social change.

Our goal is to publish books that encourage critical thinking and constructive action on the key political, cultural, social, economic, and ecological issues shaping life in the United States and in the world. In this way, we hope to give expression to a wide diversity of democratic social movements and to provide an alternative to the products of corporate publishing.

To order books, please send a check or money order to: South End Press, 7 Brookline Street, #1, Cambridge, MA 02139-4146. Or call 1-800-533-8478. Please include $3.50 for postage and handling for the first book and 50 cents for each additional book. Write or e-mail us at southend@southendpress.org for a free catalog, or visit our web site at http://www.southendpress.org.